Ambrose,

I ho[?]

As you [?]

Best p[?]

administration.

Best regards,

Henry

9-2018

SUCCESS OR FAILURE?

SUCCESS OR FAILURE?

THE UNTOLD STORY OF HEALTHCARE.GOV

HENRY CHAO

Advantage®

Published by Advantage, Charleston, South Carolina.
Member of Advantage Media Group.

ADVANTAGE is a registered trademark, and the Advantage colophon is a trademark of Advantage Media Group, Inc.

Printed in the United States of America.

10 9 8 7 6 5 4 3 2 1

ISBN: 978-1-59932-895-9
LCCN: 2018951378

Cover and layout design by Melanie Cloth.

This publication is designed to provide accurate and authoritative information in regard to the subject matter covered. It is sold with the understanding that the publisher is not engaged in rendering legal, accounting, or other professional services. If legal advice or other expert assistance is required, the services of a competent professional person should be sought.

Advantage Media Group is proud to be a part of the Tree Neutral® program. Tree Neutral offsets the number of trees consumed in the production and printing of this book by taking proactive steps such as planting trees in direct proportion to the number of trees used to print books. To learn more about Tree Neutral, please visit **www.treeneutral.com**.

Advantage Media Group is a publisher of business, self-improvement, and professional development books and online learning. We help entrepreneurs, business leaders, and professionals share their Stories, Passion, and Knowledge to help others Learn & Grow. Do you have a manuscript or book idea that you would like us to consider for publishing? Please visit **advantagefamily.com** or call **1.866.775.1696**.

DEDICATION & ACKNOWLEDGEMENTS

I considered trying to name everyone that was involved in the HealthCare.gov project but I feared that I would somehow leave someone out, not to mention that it would probably number in to the thousands of names.

All the people that dedicated their life to making October 1st happen know who they are and the role they played in one of the most complex and large-scale initiatives in the history of US health care. Many continue to devote their lives to keep the Insurance Marketplaces operational and available to millions of people as their conduit to healthcare coverage and going into the sixth open enrollment period for 2019. Whether you were or still are at the federal level, state level, local level, private sector, or contractor, it doesn't really matter because you all were in it together, focusing on delivering for day one and thereafter—fixing, stabilizing, and adjusting all that takes place year-to-year, release-to-release. It is a never ending 24/7/365 operation that demands dedicated and committed people. From my perspective at the federal level, I can honestly say that almost no one came to the organization because of pay or position—nearly everyone I've encountered considered this work as a once in a lifetime opportunity. I've even had staff that took tremendous salary cuts from their well-paying jobs outside of government just to be able to be part of a noble and meaningful effort.

This book is dedicated to all the people that stepped up to meet the October 1, 2013 challenge and those that continue to work in ensuring people have access to healthcare coverage.

TABLE OF CONTENTS

PREFACE

Throughout my career at the Centers for Medicare & Medicaid Services (CMS), I've been fortunate to work on many exciting and meaningful projects. During my first fifteen years, the experience I gained from being in the center of the storm prepared me to step away from CMS and become a part of a new chapter in the continuing saga of the US health-care system. From late 2009 to the launch of HealthCare.gov on October 1, 2013, I felt I was being tested daily on my intellectual stamina, emotional endurance, and ability to take blow after blow.

No matter how many times I fell down or was at my wits end struggling to come up with a way to continue towards the objective of the Healthcare.gov launch, I had to get back up and figure out how to get through another day; not so much for myself, but for the collective "we" who would benefit from a new way of making healthcare coverage available in our healthcare landscape, especially for those who needed it most. Being a leader in the effort meant I had to show resilience and persevere without losing sight of the objective.

Yes, I knew there would be significant challenges that would seem insurmountable. I foresaw online, real-time enrollment in health-care coverage, with all the underlying and necessary foundational pieces, as not just being a new user experience, but also very complex, making it more challenging to understand for the average uninsured applicant. This was exacerbated by a "big bang" implementation rather than a phased approach, resulting in a far less than perfect launch. But, on a more personal level, launching the program under these circumstances by the established date of October 1, 2013 meant that we could never go back; no retreat, no pause, no reset to rethink another solution.

To get started, we focused on the most basic, fundamental aspect of Healthcare.gov: enrollment. Enrollment means that the consumer must have the ability to choose from an array of health plans that are available in their area and then process the appropriate information to get them enrolled. Once we could get this first step done where people and families were enrolled in coverage, the next logical steps are to accommodate those applicants that encountered issues and improve the experience of an online enrollment process.

Getting to October 1st with a functioning product, where the prior years of work was converging on that single date, meant that we were all racing to the starting line, not the finish line. In large scale programs, including the Insurance Marketplaces, systems do not stay static; no software is ever perfect when it is released because the underlying business needs that it supports is continuously evolving.

Prior to the launch, several of my team members, both federal staff and government contractors, commented that I should write a book given the grueling effort to make progress day-to-day. We all laughed about how to best tell the story; whether to include moments where logic and reason were suspended, but somehow, we took the most illogical and unbelievable circumstances and made it work, including schedule changes, rearranging the sequence of priorities based on politics, issuing policies without any details, not allowing technical information to be shared openly to stakeholders—the list goes on and on.

I contemplated taking on the task of telling a story that has dozens of angles, perspectives, subtext, and more importantly, to help others comprehend the experience by setting the proper context in which all this happened. Context always matters because it helps explain why things happen the way they do, no matter how illogical it may seem when you replay the events. Particularly in a different context, such as after the fact, superimposing selected events, without the constraints and urgency, contributed greatly in shaping the outcome.

When I was the Chief Technology Officer at CMS, my team and I would conduct lifecycle reviews in which project teams would present their plans for design, development, testing, implementation, and operations. The forum is called the Technical Review Board (TRB) and it continues to exist in CMS today as an effective checkpoint to ensure standards and best practices are adhered to and will not jeopardize the entire enterprise. These reviews were conducted "tabletop" style in which the main artifact used PowerPoint presentations where architectural renderings, data flows, interfaces, etc. are all diagrammed from a conceptual level down to the detailed implementation level.

In conducting these reviews, I often remarked that "everything works in PowerPoint." These reviews, while necessary, can only ponder the theory of how it will work when deployed as an integrated system and not the reality of what will happen upon deployment—theory versus reality. I hope to convey how they were very different in the planning and execution of Healthcare.gov by October 1st and that the best of intentions, knowledge, and experience still must meet the expectations and edicts set largely by the Legislative Branch, Judicial Branch, and Executive Branch between 2009 and 2014.

INTRODUCTION

During the month of November 2013, much of my time was spent meeting with congressional committee staffers to be interviewed and deposed, working with various Department of Health & Human Services (HHS) staff to coordinate messaging prior to going to the Hill, and preparing for and testifying before congressional committees on issues about the status of HealthCare.gov. Republican committee staffers loved to ask the same questions, just worded differently, to try and catch me off guard and see if I would provide inconsistent answers. I had to balance delicately between being honest and truthful on the one hand, and patient and accommodating on the other, since the atmosphere was more like a "guilty until proven innocent" interrogation.

Being deposed by staffers and testifying before Congress is extremely intimidating even in the best circumstances. After the first two to three engagements, I settled in and realized that whatever anyone wanted to ask and however they asked it, my responses would be always truthful and consistent. That's because I was one of the few people who had been with the Insurance Marketplace program from before the passage of the Senate version of the ACA bill to the October 1, 2013 launch.

The term "Insurance Exchange" was originally used in the Senate version of the bill that later became known as the Patient Protection and Affordable

Care Act (PPACA, or as most refer to it as, ACA). The term "Insurance Marketplace" is synonymous with "Insurance Exchange," but the former was widely used starting in 2012 in marketing and promotional efforts to build public awareness of the impending change to how most insured people would purchase health insurance.

I was in a unique position of being able to explain the events that took place and how things unfolded for this unprecedented change in US health care. How did I get here? What had transpired to that point in time? To maintain my perspective, I'd replay the key events that ran in serial or in parallel. Those events helped me answer the barrage of questions from the friendlies and not-so-friendlies on the panel.

Since I was a member of the executive branch representing the work done on the Insurance Marketplace program, in all the backroom sessions and testimony open to the public I was poked, prodded, and insulted as part of this great initiative. But in my mind, I knew I was there because we had done something remarkable. Most reasonable people in nonpolitically dramatized circumstances would agree—in principle at least—that expanding access to health-care coverage is good public policy and not some dastardly government deed to subversively try to help people have access to health care. We had begun to change the American health-care system—and creating an online platform for people to use in signing up for coverage was only the beginning.

Rather than feeling only the pressure and stress of having to answer for the messy rollout, I decided to embrace these inquisitions into HealthCare.gov. I began to think of the appearances before Congress as a privilege and opportunity to take a stand for the work that hundreds, if not thousands, performed to launch the program in spite of the extreme constraints placed on the project.

There is never a spot in your career where you say to yourself, "Hey, one day, I want to be in the hot seat testifying before a congressional committee." Yet there I was, doing exactly that. As I sat there, I had to continually ask myself: "What is the risk?" Was it a personal risk, or was it a risk to the current presidential administration? Ultimately, I found it was a risk to both.

The sessions I'm referring to were intended to capitalize on the very messy and public rollout of HealthCare.gov and to further fan the flames of criticism of the ACA, commonly known as Obamacare. I was the deputy chief information officer (CIO) for CMS at the time, working with my closest advisors to design the architecture of the systems behind HealthCare.gov.

It is indeed the natural behavior of an investigative body to dig up names and challenge the people before them in their tribunals. That is what was going on when I was being grilled with questions by the chair and Republican members of the House Committee on what many of us in the executive branch fondly refer to as *ogre* (a derivation of OGR, or Oversight and Government Reform). We needed to maintain our humor in the face of what we considered a senseless investigation.

Beyond humor, we also needed to be prepared. We didn't walk into the tribunal cold; we had weeks of preparation. We might have been put through the grinder, but we were already aged and seasoned before that process began. With so many interested parties, including some who set out to attack it from the start, we knew what a super-political controversy the national health-care rollout entailed.

Now that all is said and done, I want to set the record straight—to tell my part of the story. That is why I decided to write this book.

THE BIG PICTURE

Those moments when I and my work were on trial might seem like a low point to anyone who doesn't understand the big picture. Instead, they represented a position of strength—defending what I consider was one of the greatest and noblest efforts in implementing a much-needed public policy change, and being a part of the effort overseeing the technical implementation of what may be the most challenging endeavor in the history of the US health-care system, was indeed a privilege.

I was the government's principal senior executive leader for the technical implementation of the ACA's Insurance Marketplace program, which later became more commonly referred to as Health-Care.gov. While most refer to HealthCare.gov as "just a website," few knew what was behind the centerpiece and public interface of President Barack Obama's historic health-care legislation. Many of those against the act, Mr. Issa included, referred to all of ACA as "Obamacare," as if labeling a major piece of legislation with the name of its progenitor would fuel the disdain of people who do not agree that health care should be a right in this great country.

Beyond all the stories told to date, this book is about my perspective built on years of public service that led to the launch of HealthCare.gov, and on providing a first hand account of what it takes to launch such an initiative in hopes of dispelling the notion that government cant get things done. Granted, my book is part memoir—again, a chance to set the record straight. Yet, it is also a way to show the value and personal reward of a life dedicated to public service within the framework of a democratic government.

It is about making our world a better place through increased access to health care for all Americans, an issue that continues to be debated.

My book has several goals, and is aimed at:

- anyone interested in the ACA who has kept up with the news and continues to have interest in information about what can be learned for future endeavors of similar complexity and scale;

- the average person who understands how technology, when properly applied, can be extremely beneficial, but can't reconcile why, in situations like HealthCare.gov, it can be so mishandled. So often in very large scale, complex initiatives, technology isn't the source of the problem but is the easiest to shine a spotlight on to illustrate what went wrong. For this audience, I hope to significantly broaden the ability to holistically examine and understand the range and depth of all the issues involved in implementing a complex program;

- the hearts and minds of stakeholders within the technology field along with its opinion leaders, from bloggers to journalists. I want to help this group understand what appeared to go wrong and where government can be made more efficient when it comes to implementing technology;

- anyone involved in large-scale projects, in the public or private sector, struggling to make forward progress in an atmosphere of chaotic decision making and seeking assurances that they are not alone in their experiences; and

- public servants who have wearily adopted a "no good deed goes unpunished" outlook on how much positive change they can personally lead and influence in a public service environment that does not encourage taking calculated risks, when so often that's exactly what's needed.

Ultimately, this book is an ode to the concept of public service and what can be accomplished by government when it seeks to help people—an issue that continues to resonate for America, regardless of who is in power—and to fuel the belief that it only takes a small handful of people to create positive change in the world we live in.

ULTIMATELY, THIS BOOK IS AN ODE TO THE CONCEPT OF PUBLIC SERVICE AND WHAT CAN BE ACCOMPLISHED BY GOVERNMENT WHEN IT SEEKS TO HELP PEOPLE

In our case, despite the challenges, the public "good" that we set about to create was put in place as promised, although it was far from perfect. Still, I want to let everyone, regardless of political party or public or private sector affiliation, know how the process can be made more efficient. I'm certain that looking behind the scenes with the curtains pulled back will reveal the truth behind the headlines. Telling the story from my perspective will allow you to understand what it means to be committed, to embrace your own fate as part of the commitment, to remain focused while maneuvering through uncertainty, and to stay true to what you know in your heart and mind to be the best course in the journey. In my case, that journey was to implement the provisions of the law, to the best of my ability, so that people who qualified to be covered under ACA had a means to enroll in health-care coverage.

DAMAGE CONTROL: MANAGING THE MESSAGE

At the time the HealthCare.gov launch was being challenged, I was with CMS, an agency within HHS.

While the standard chain of command was that I reported at the agency level, several layers of senior people at HHS were involved during the hearings, including the department's general counsel, assistant secretaries, legislative affairs personnel, and the like.

Each of these groups wanted to advise me on how to best answer questions. The preparation was no different from being deposed by an attorney as part of litigation—I was reminded of what I needed to say and how I should say it.

First and foremost, of course, is telling the truth. Congressional committees have subpoena powers, along with being both judge and jury. If you are held in contempt or caught lying to Congress, you can be jailed. In the midst of all the "training" to be consistent in providing truthful answers, I was told: if given the choice of admitting you are lying or admitting you are stupid, always say you're stupid. That pragmatic piece of advice was a wakeup call about how serious the situation was.

But in going through the preparation processes, I discovered that those around me were positioning for the lowest risk to themselves. Each group wanted to highlight different levels of detail, some more technical, others more policy. They helped me prep in each area of their concern, not so much because they were worried about my future, but because they were worried about the future of the process, the organization, and the administration. General counsel and department staff were not helping me prepare because they were genuinely concerned about my destiny. Rather, they were tactfully shaping testimony so that I did not conclude the hearing in a way that resulted in additional people being subpoenaed. The objective was to curb the witch hunt tactics the committee was accused of.

Make no mistake: there were some very good people in the process. A few with the CMS Office of Legislation were my "tour guides" every time I went to the Hill. They were quite helpful and accommodating in informing me about how the process worked. They were cheerleaders of a sort, escorting me to the Hill and giving me moral support beyond their duties. In contrast to those who tended to maintain a safe distance while feeling me out for what I was going to do, that handful of friendlies understood that I was genuinely trying to do my job. So they shared with me the etiquette and protocols I needed to ensure that my voice was heard.

IT TOOK MORE STAMINA TO SPEAK FOR THE WORK THAN TO DO THE WORK

In the months preceding the October 2013 launch of HealthCare.gov and for several months afterward, I had been through three hearings, accompanied by multiple prep sessions, backroom depositions, and meetings with certain Congressional representatives and their staff. The first, in July 2013, I was tasked to accompany Marilyn Tavenner, our administrator at the time, to a hearing. I served as a support person, sitting next to her at the hearing to help answer questions.

These hearings have a specific etiquette that might be a mystery to anyone watching them on television on CNN or C-SPAN. Basically, anyone with a nameplate in front of them is in the hot seat. In the first row behind the hot seat are the people to ask for immediate advice, and additional support people sit in the rows behind them.

Despite the support and seeming regimentation, the process is still one involving an unknown, something you must go through to truly understand. It's like bungee jumping for the first time; there's a safety mechanism, but you don't know what it feels like until you make the jump. The only thing you know is that if something goes wrong, it's a long way down. You have faith that the rope will bring you back up to safety.

Yet each time, it does get easier. With each subsequent hearing, you have a sense of what it is like, including which interested stakeholders have their own best interests in mind versus those considering yours. But you must take that first leap into the unknown to get there.

With me, there was always some level of fear in what I would say, because it is in my nature to communicate with people and help them understand what's going on. So I was constantly coached to be more conservative in what I would offer up. I also had a reputation not only for speaking my mind but also for being a little irreverent. Case in point: Todd Park, who at the time was the reigning chief technology officer (CTO) for the federal government—and was also a close ally and collaborator tracking the progress and issues of the federal IT efforts for the Insurance Marketplaces—often joined me in meetings with other top officials at the Office of Management and Budget (OMB). We'd all gather in a room and they'd grill me with questions, which were more focused on technical issues that paled in comparison to other burning issues with policy development and lack of clarity and guidance on business requirements. After one such meeting, Todd gave me some advice: "Two things," he said. "One, try not to be so indignant when you're answering questions. And two, you should try to answer the question people ask you, not the question that you think people should be asking you."

That might have seemed like good advice in the OMB context, but I had real work to do to solve problems unique to the Insurance Marketplaces, of which, in my mind, were higher priorities than to listen to people giving good advice, but good in the specific context they were referring to. I was constantly being summoned to answer questions and to explain what was actually involved in implementing something much more complex and on a scale unlike what many people tried to equivocate with using their experiences. Questions came from stakeholder communities ranging from Congressional Committees, OMB staffers, industry associations, and other federal and state agencies. While some were quite substantive and to the point in identifying what was needed or missing in how we were sharing information, many other questions were all over the place with analogs that really were not apples-to-apples comparisons—questions comparing running a tech start-up, local government setting up 211 hotlines for reporting potholes, and managing a gaming platform launch, to name a few. While I appreciated the sharing of experiences, I sensed that these were not bidirectional conversations about good ideas. Nor did the most of the people offering advice appreciated the full range of constraints that very few understand about the lengthy and labyrinthine process by which the government notifies the public of its policy intentions. That process includes publication of draft and final regulations and solicitations of public comments. Those are not so much from private citizens but rather mostly from affected industry organizations and businesses, such as insurance companies in the case of the ACA.

The constraints also included the Federal Acquisition Regulation (FAR), agency local procurement policies, mountains of technical debt—the accumulation of previously implemented short term solutions that no one ever went back and optimized for the long term—that exists in every agency, and integration challenges where capabilities needed for new programs collided with existing legacy systems, data, processes, and operations. We were charged to build an online, real-time eligibility and enrollment system with significant integrations with legacy data and systems owned by the Internal Revenue Service (IRS), the Social Security Administration (SSA), the Department of Homeland Security (DHS), the Department of Defense (DoD), the Department of Veterans Affairs (VA), and several other agencies, as well as with every state's Medicaid and CHIP programs, the state insurance commissioners, and hundreds of insurance companies that are licensed by each state to "issue" policies that provide health-care coverage—and it all had to be coordinated to produce a "world-class experience" for consumers. No one had ever tackled such a task. No one had ever even witnessed anything with that level of detail, called for everything from policy translation at all legislative levels, to requirements that could actually be given to people to design and develop systems, to choosing the right technologies to architect and integrate in order to engineer and implement a solution.

Keep in mind that one of the major tasks I was expected to perform was to answer any questions levied by anyone who had a legitimate stake in the effort. Since that was one of my core job functions, I was more than happy to explain to any level of detail necessary to help others understand the challenges. But when questions asked were clearly from an ill-informed perspective—and regardless of how tactfully I tried to help someone arrive at their own revelation of what was at hand—I often felt like I was dealing with a five-year-old asking, "but why, but why, but why?" So I got a little indignant when I had to keep answering the same questions over and over with reworded answers.

A great example is a question I was asked by the first director of the Office of Consumer Information and Insurance Oversight (OCIIO) after having put together a draft budget, a five-year outlook of the costs of systems—enrollment, payment, financial management, and others—to stand up the Marketplace for all the states. "Why does the IT cost so much?" he asked, which I answered by explaining the breakdown of each system—what it did, the types of data it handled, the level of security and privacy implications, and so on. But no matter how many times I explained it, he couldn't understand the numbers, because he couldn't fathom the pieces that were involved. It was like trying to explain how health insurance really works in the United States to someone who has never had health insurance coverage.

Finally, I got to where, in answers to his questions about any particular detail, I would just read back the key points of the legislation that called for it, such as calculation of advance premium tax credits (APTCs) or the need to verify against federal authoritative sources. Since I was citing nontechnical aspects of the requirements referred to in the law, I was speaking his language. Even though my answers still didn't adequately describe the IT costs, he became more comfortable that my answers were at least staying in his realm of comprehension, since we were no longer speaking about technology. While I don't want to come across as harsh or arrogant, I try to meet people halfway by trying to comprehend what I do not know or understand. I either do my homework or at least take a leap of faith that the person who is trying to explain something to me knows what they're talking about. When there's no give and take and the conversation moves entirely to one person's comfort zone, there's small chance of truly understanding the issues.

People seek answers to their questions because they want a greater level of comfort to understand how things are going. But they ask the questions within their frame of experience and knowledge, and when they hear things they don't recognize, it makes them uneasy. Rather than trying to meet you halfway, they begin to dig in more, and then they feel almost like not cooperating. Caution had to be exercised when dealing with senior, high-level policy people who were politically affiliated. They were not in their positions to tackle all the problems of the health-care system, but rather, they were laser-focused on the established political agenda and on executing that agenda—that was their top priority.

In many cases, the political agenda uncovered various inefficiencies and other established priorities that had been in play for many years—for example, the fifty-plus years of established Medicare and Medicaid policies, systems, and operations and their interdependencies. Trying to implement a new national-scale, complex program with tremendous interdependencies on top of what already existed in the US health-care landscape created significant challenges to established priorities, resources, commitments, and of course, any previously made, less-than-optimal decisions.

Trying to explain how the political agenda and priorities of the day had to balance with what already existed was a delicate conversation to have. How do you create appreciation for the risk created by the "disruption" of a new program to existing agency operations without sounding unsupportive of the new program?

When the Republicans resoundingly won the House majority in the 2010 midterms, the OCIIO and its programs were moved to CMS. From the perspective of CMS, there was great concern over how to feed another hungry mouth when it didn't even have enough resources (budgets, people, facilities) to fulfill its responsibilities under the ACA. On the surface, there was full cooperation to find the necessary resources to make some forward progress, but beneath the thin layer of cooperation and support were some Herculean struggles to adequately fund contracts, hire the right people, and determine who would make the call on trade-offs between Medicare, Medicaid, and Marketplace programs. It's one thing to inform the senior executives that run the agency that new priorities have been determined. It's another thing to battle the inertia that exists from institutionalized processes that were not created to be highly adaptive to rapidly changing circumstances—namely budgeting, contracting, hiring, and publishing regulations, which all move at their own levels of urgency.

When you are part of a new program with wide-reaching implications across numerous major federal agencies and programs, the first reaction is rarely a welcome with wide-open arms and offers of immediate assistance. No. You're a new zebra with different stripes, and every other member of the herd is concerned about the unknown nature of the new arrival. Everyone wants to know what they're going to lose by having this new member around. In fact, your efforts can be branded as risky and threatening to the cultural norms.

That is how the entire ACA and its more than four hundred sections were distilled down to "Obamacare." The goal was to equate anything bad with the law to President Obama. For example, the federal Data Services Hub (DSH) that my team and I developed to fulfill a key missing aspect of federal authoritative data sources, which were limited in their real-time capabilities—such as being used for eligibility verification during an online consumer session—was generally met with skepticism and fear. While that had not been done before in the context of national-scale online enrollments, it was certainly necessary given that the alternative was to access the data in non-real time, which would kill the entire proposition. It would seem the concept would be embraced, especially by those who clearly understood the problem at hand. Rather than all the participating agencies and OMB jumping in and collectively owning the concept, for at least the entire first year it was generally referred to as "Henry's Hub"—as if to ensure the personal branding would allow for participation from a safe distance if anything were to go wrong and someone at the top demanded to see who came up with the idea. With my name as part of the concept, obviously that wouldn't be anyone else. Trust me, when that kind of thing happens, it doesn't happen because people are appreciative of such a novel idea. It happens as a matter of managing one's own risk exposure.

Similarly, I was given wild titles like "project manager for HealthCare.gov" or "the architect for Obamacare" by people trying to categorize and understand the boundaries in which I operated. When leading an effort of great magnitude, it isn't just about the work you do in directing staff and contractors; half of the work clearly is managing upwards and across the universe of stakeholders. You have to be very resilient, know who you are, and command the truth to keep from tripping over yourself. If there's any crack in your armor, they're going to try to exploit it. Clearly, I wasn't just designing, architecting, or managing resources and delivering the Marketplace program. I was also required to be the voice and the resource of knowledge and information about how things transpired.

CHAPTER 1

A MIND FOR PROBLEM-SOLVING

My path has long been one of public service, but it was serendipitous at first. When I reflect back, I think about the opening scene of "Forrest Gump," where all that is onscreen is a feather floating in the wind, waiting to land somewhere, only to move again with every breeze. You might believe you are making the decisions about your destiny, good, bad or otherwise, but something is carrying you along the way.

One component of that unseen force toward public service was the concept that there's a natural binding social fabric that evolves when people agree to accomplish things that serve more than just their own needs. That sense of evolving for a greater good is a powerful attraction for many, and sometimes it isn't obvious that it is the force that drives them. Think of people who work in law enforcement, first responders, and so many other noble professions in which people run toward danger rather than away from it. Sometimes that force is subtler and manifests as a desire to nurture others to realize their own calling—educators or people who work with others dealing with daily challenges come to mind.

I grew up in a very close-knit family that felt that drive. My father taught physical education and was more of the active type, while my mother taught art and piano and was more of the artistic type. We lived with my maternal grandparents in a house where art flourished, as my grandmother was a teacher of Ikebana, the Japanese art of flower arrangement. In that house, I was constantly exposed to people who were not true relatives, but were close friends treated like relatives and given titles of endearment such as "uncle," "aunt," "brother," and "sister." My family was a part of the community, always extending themselves socially and intellectually, which helped teach me to appreciate diversity and to be a more open and receptive person when working with people.

Through my maternal grandfather, I was also exposed to public service at an early age. My grandfather was a government public servant, an elder statesman to whom people often turned to for advice. In our home, he was the enforcer of etiquette and manners, and when I was around him, I always had to follow protocol, be very respectful, and speak only when spoken to. Through those experiences, I learned to understand my surroundings and the context in which I was more mindful of others around me and what kind of situation I was in.

People who work in public service generally have social and nonsocial events, meeting large numbers of other people. In this sense, I was carried by the wind at an early age, meeting many people, realizing also what it was to be of service to others and to help people from the position of government. At the time, I did not realize that the best thing in life is to be in service of others, yet it was always in the background, a concept programmed into me from childhood.

Along with an innate desire to serve, I've always had a problem-solving nature. Even as a child, I was attracted to complex problems. I liked to disassemble things and figure out how they worked. I always got in trouble because I'd take apart everything in the house and then put it back together. So it stood to reason that anytime something was broken, it was likely because of something I had done.

Those two pieces of my personality would serve me well in the role that I undertook as part of the HealthCare.gov rollout. It also helped that part of me is always feeling and sensing the world around me and trying to figure out what makes life interesting, while another part of me is more about the hardline, physical realities of science, engineering, project schedules, and costs when it comes to managing resources and people. It's a funny blend, but one that helped me make some very tough decisions in very extreme circumstances.

The floating feather demonstrates how even through sheer self-determination, few individuals arrive at a particular point in life all on their own. Other things are always acting on us to help shape who we are, who we become. The idea that service to country and people was something that could fuel my motivation while also being a rewarding experience revealed itself to me as I was trying to figure out what to do. Many people have a moment in their lives making choices not because they know what they want to do, but because they know they need to be on a different path.

When you are floating around a little too much, society makes you feel like you're wandering aimlessly. I did a little of that until I ultimately decided that I would benefit from a disciplined and structured organization, which led me to enlist in the Navy in 1984. The military provides an abundance of hands-on training in a variety of skills, everything you need to know in support of the "mission." The experience is fast paced, a process where you are always acquiring new knowledge and each individual with a role to play in service to something greater than any single individual.

A MILITARY EDUCATION—TURNING ABSTRACT INTO PRACTICE

Military service progressively teaches how to handle more responsibility by going from academics to practice very quickly; practice is what—as much as possible—keeps people safe in the military. So much of dealing with public policy is a little abstract, but someone has to figure out how to turn that abstraction into real physical ways of implementing programs—and having been through military training that forces you to quickly adapt the academics to a real-world situation helps in that regard.

To do that, military training puts you directly into the environment you are being prepared for. For example, firefighting is not learned only in the classroom. Instead, after the classroom portion of the training the military throws you, along with a firefighting team and equipment, into a room simulating the lower decks of a ship with diesel fuel lit under you. Suddenly you're standing in the middle of a thousand-degree fire learning how to put it out. That kind of realism coupled with the theory of firefighting aboard a ship helps you better understand the possibilities of a situation. The experiential side of military training gives a sense of extreme realism not always seen in civilian life, providing you a direct, first hand glimpse in to how good or how bad something can be.

The first five years of my military career, I served as an avionics technician on the aircraft carrier *USS Enterprise*. My job was to troubleshoot and repair malfunctioning avionics—systems such as navigation, anti-submarine warfare, radio communications, radar, infrared cameras, and electronic countermeasures used by various aircraft deployed with the carrier. Understanding how to fix massively complex avionics equipment on board an aircraft carrier that sometimes cruises nonstop for three months straight at sea means you have to do your part in knowing how to be self-sufficient in maintaining maximum mission-capable status on all the operating aircraft. In order to achieve that, you have to ensure that everything in the supply chain is fully optimized so you have the right specifications, parts, documentation, and absolutely every last detail addressed.

As a result, the Navy taught me the practice of "integrated logistics," which I have applied in many other aspects of my career, especially in always having full knowledge of the supply chain and backup plans, and in just being resourceful and anticipatory of all possible conditions in order to mitigate as many as possible under my control.

But especially in operations, things don't always go as intended. Servicing an aircraft in the Navy requires an awareness of and familiarity with the entire assembly of the aircraft, including all of its internal and external support systems, and even the aircraft carrier itself—a vessel that is handled by nearly six thousand officers and crew members. Each has a respective role to play in an operationally intense environment where the combined skill sets and experience hold top-down and bottom-up views of integrated systems that work together to serve the mission of the Navy. In this environment, an avionics technician armed with years of classroom and hands-on experience is expected to always properly troubleshoot and fix problems regardless of the situation. For instance, even though billions of dollars are spent on integrated logistics to ensure the availability of everything needed to sustain a carrier-based aircraft in the middle of the ocean, sometimes that system doesn't accommodate first-time kinds of problems. So one learns to be very resourceful in very dire situations—the same skills needed to fix the systems and data problems in health-care programs.

In short, the Navy provided what was essentially a "full life cycle" view and first-person experience, from basic training to survive on a ship and at sea, to the theory, design, and engineering of the equipment that I worked on, to connecting with the real-world aspects of maintaining aircraft aboard an aircraft carrier. That holistic macro-to-micro experience of the interdependencies involved in producing the intended result of a mission that I was an integral part of provided me with the knowledge, awareness, and confidence to be able to take something from an idea to implementation and every-thing necessary in between to support the implementation.

To this day, I still retain the strong desire to grasp the big picture. I want to understand it well enough to align all the necessary pieces and dependencies in order to deliver an intended outcome. In the case of the ACA, the big picture was so much more than what was debated and attacked as "Obamacare."

Being part of an aircraft carrier's operational intensity served me well in a 24/7 health-care environment that required immediate action to fix, repair, and mitigate when an issue arose—in essence, doing whatever it took to achieve the minimum necessary to start and continue the operation and be ready to handle the next series of issues. Resourcefulness, appreciation for the possible, perseverance, and commitment are the lessons that carry forward, and in many ways, came from a truly trial-by-fire set of experiences that provided me the strength to weather the most difficult situations. Taking on the goals of the ACA seemed a natural next step in my somewhat internally guided, somewhat serendipitous journey to be part of something much bigger than myself.

TRANSITIONING FROM SEA DUTY TO SHORE DUTY

After five years serving as an avionics technician aboard the *USS Enterprise*, my sea duty service requirement was met and it was time to transition to shore duty. I spoke to a Navy detailer whose duty was to ensure the Navy's needs were met first while providing me with options on the job and location I might have in a shore-based assignment. I wanted to move from the West Coast to the East Coast to be closer to my parents in New York, but in 1989, the military began downsizing, and coast-to-coast changes were costly and tougher to arrange. So I transitioned to shore duty, first taking a nearly yearlong assignment to attend "C" school for intermediate avionics in Millington, Tennessee. After that, I took an assignment as a member of a hybrid Navy and civilian "reliability and maintainability" team stationed at the Naval Air Warfare Center in Lexington Park, Maryland. I worked alongside civilian engineers and staff from the Integrated Logistics Program Office who were managing the avionics suite transition from a fleet of C-130 aircraft to a fleet of Boeing 707 aircraft. Being stationed in southern Maryland allowed for me to frequently visit my parents in New York and to settle into a more stable schedule to start a family.

Finally, after ten years in the military, I decided it was time to move on. That was a momentous year: I graduated summa cum laude with a bachelor's degree in economics from St. Mary's College of Maryland, my first daughter, Grace, was born, and I decided to transition from the military into government employment. A number of people tried to convince me to stay in the military, reasoning that with another ten years of service I could retire. But to me, that meant another ten years before I could start another life. I also didn't want to go back out to sea now that I had started a family. It was an extremely difficult decision to make, because after investing ten years and to a great degree being comfortable and familiar with the "military family," it was quite scary to step outside of that predictable comfort zone and shift into an unknown future.

I eventually applied for and was offered a position as a health insurance specialist at the Health Care Financing Administration (HCFA) in the summer of 1994, and I accepted the offer to start as a GS-7, which is an entry level pay grade in the Division of State Systems in the Medicaid Bureau of the Health Care Financing Administration (HCFA), which in 2001, was renamed the Centers for Medicare & Medicaid Services (CMS).

EXPERIENCE LAYS THE GROUNDWORK

Rick Friedman was the director for the Division of State Systems and the person who hired me after a phone interview. For the next ten years, I worked under Rick and learned how to better communicate and build relationships within CMS, with other federal and state agencies, and health care industry associations. While I greatly appreciated his hands-off style in letting his staff find the best ways to solve problems, every so often that appreciation turned to frustration, because achieving any level of change meant breaking down institutional barriers myself, which really benefitted me in the long run in terms of self-sufficiency. Rick's "light touch" management style allowed me to learn, participate, engage, and lead various interesting efforts undertaken by the division. From 1994 to about 2004, I was involved in many interesting projects, including: driving wide adoption of health care electronic data interchange (EDI) standards, Y2K independent validation & verification (IV&V) efforts to ensure readiness in the state Medicaid programs, and building a grassroots effort to bring enterprise architecture (EA) practices to how states planned and executed their technology investments. The latter of these, the Medicaid IT architecture framework (MITA), has matured to become a key part of how states are funded for their IT projects and measured for their alignment with the MITA principles.

Rick's style of managing stakeholder expectations, his approach to getting people to engage, listen, and participate, and his ultra-smooth, eloquent delivery of information had a strong influence in how I managed myself in various situations as a representative of the federal government. For instance, I learned to be highly sensitive to senior state-level executive's time when I was standing in "regulator" shoes and trying to get them to accept the federal government's policy and direction—particularly when there was significant skepticism that the government would add value beyond approving funding for the state to award IT contracts and conduct day-to-day operations, but also to know when to stand my ground in executing my obligations as a regulator.

I flourished in learning and thinking big picture under Rick. He allowed me to take responsibility for and own both successes and failures. Working for Rick and being exposed to a wide range of experiences—from leading a project through concept to implementation, to managing myself and other people's expectations—were the initial practical lessons I acquired in a journey that eventually led to being part of the ACA Insurance Marketplace rollout.

The federal side of the Medicaid program, where I started my new career, was perhaps the best place to quickly be immersed in some of the core issues with the US health-care system. The federal part of the Medicaid program provides for matching funds to every state, the District of Columbia, and US territories for the costs of health care expenditures, administration and operation of the program, and acquiring, operating, and maintaining the supporting systems. State governments, and to a great degree, county governments, are on the front lines of Medicaid in their respective jurisdictions, working with people who are applying for benefits. For example, determining a person or family's eligibility for health care is perhaps one of the most operationally complex aspects of the US health-care system, and of the various ways to become eligible for health-care coverage in a particular state, Medicaid is certainly one of the more complex programs. Medicaid eligibility rules are different in every state, and changes are fairly frequent. Changes are often driven by new or revised federal and/or state legislation and occasionally by court rulings, such as in 2012 when the US Supreme Court struck down the provision of the ACA that would have had every state expand Medicaid eligibility rules. While states do share basic rules of eligibility, the Medicaid program was designed to allow flexibility for states to manage the program based on their demographics, budgets, priorities, social and economic factors, and legislative agendas.

Working in the Medicaid program also taught me the necessity to understand and appreciate the dynamics between the states, counties, and federal government. The diversity and frequent cycles of change make it challenging to implement and operate systems. The operational tempo of the Medicaid programs and level of resourcefulness required by state and county staff to ensure that people are receiving the benefits they qualify for is similar to the operational tempo and level of resourcefulness required in the Navy when trying to ensure the safety of aviators and their crew and shipmates in highly arduous conditions. In health care, particularly, the can-do attitude of the people on the public service frontlines in the states and counties was a constant reminder that there is a greater good that ordinary people can contribute to.

In many ways, the skills, training, and exposure to the operational tempo aboard an aircraft carrier for five years followed by integrated logistics and project management support for five years was quite applicable to working at CMS. The critical, structured thinking, the ability to decompose a large problem into smaller parts, and then the

ULTIMATELY, THIS BOOK IS AN ODE TO THE CONCEPT OF PUBLIC SERVICE AND WHAT CAN BE ACCOMPLISHED BY GOVERNMENT WHEN IT SEEKS TO HELP PEOPLE

solution of those problems at the micro level and their reconstitution back at the larger, macro level, were all very similar.

As time went on, the aging workforce at HCFA that was moving on toward retirement was transferring institutional knowledge to newbies like me, and I was soaking it all up like a sponge. However, the process for transferring knowledge was not always efficient. Almost daily, the old guard presented me with piles of documents outlining rules and regulations, along with system diagrams and concept papers, while saying, "You need to learn this because I might not be here in a couple weeks."

Through it all, it was crucial to maintain a problem-solving attitude, employ critical thinking, think on my feet, and patiently understand my role. I was a thirty-four-year old with ten years' worth of high-pressure military experience, yet I was still tactfully acquiring knowledge and learning when to speak. As a result, people began to trust me and put me in stressful situations where a more experienced person might normally be placed.

In my effort to understand the relationship between the macro and micro views within the greater ecosystem in HCFA/CMS programs, I became increasingly inquisitive. At times, I had to ignore the noise of people who were territorial or suspicious of my motives in wanting to acquire more knowledge.

Still, I was never discouraged. I was prepared to go to the ends of the earth, if necessary, to understand the macro view of our agency's various roles in the US health-care system and to be able to reconcile how changes to technology and design at the micro level can be best coordinated and executed across the numerous stakeholders that individually have their respective pieces of the puzzle.

TRAINING FOR LEADERSHIP

Within CMS, moving from a mid-level management position overseeing potentially several projects and ten to twenty-five staff into the more senior management levels such as the Senior Executive Service nets you a really valuable training opportunity—a month-long residency program called "Leadership for a Democratic Society" that takes place at the Federal Executive Institute (FEI) in Charlottesville, Virginia. This is not your average passive course on management principles with textbook examples of what leadership looks like in action. While it certainly does do some of that, the first two weeks are all about breaking you down and getting you to ask yourself some tough questions about who you are, where you came from, and where you think you might be going, especially in terms of what you would or maybe should accomplish while holding a senior position in government. The second two weeks are about immersing a deconstructed and hopefully somewhat humbler you in the fundamentals of good government, what happens when there are really bad leaders, and your role as a public servant—one who does not blindly execute orders with zero compassion and complete dispassion about the people being served. Participants visit different government offices to study concepts of civil society, equality, and rights as defined in our Constitution and Bill of Rights, as well as historically relevant examples of leadership such as Gettysburg, and practical lessons such as how to work with Congress.

Visiting the National Holocaust Museum for a workshop was a component of my lessons. It was eye-opening to realize that many people believe that the Holocaust was perpetrated mostly by the German military involved in the death camps. The lessons revealed the massive scale of collusion that had to take place within Germany's civilian agencies in order to carry out Hitler's policies to wipe from the face of the earth so many millions of Jews and non-Jews as if they had never existed, including land records, personal property, and houses. Everything had to be altered. Without the massive scale of government collusion, there could not have been such an organized conspiracy to commit genocide at that scale. It is a chilling and eye-opening fact of history that all who work in government should examine what it is that they are actually a part of. What is the overall machinery of government accomplishing? What is your role in that machinery? Nazi Germany is one of the most organized examples of genocide and represents the supreme example of government gone awry, and many would ask how it can possibly compare to the government we currently have in the United States. It's really not a comparison at all. But it is an ultra-realistic example of what happens when people don't question what it is that they actually do. It is a sobering example of what happens in government when people blindly execute the orders of the day and do not look beyond what they are told to do.

Without recognizing your role in the bigger picture, without figuring out how the work you're doing affects others, you could find yourself in situations where your work is part of a process that you find morally reprehensible. That's the key to never blindly saying, "I was only following orders." At some point, a person must ask what is going on around them.

Over the years, working on some of the largest and most complex IT projects in CMS, I heard on many occasions phrases such as "stay within the guardrails" or "stay within your swim lane." Often these were statements to ensure the IT side didn't get ahead of other pieces of a project or get into places it should not be. In fact, it's often said in the IT profession, "Business comes before IT"—in other words, IT should always stay subservient and nonthreatening to the business side. There is significant fear that IT will go off on its own to build IT for IT's sake, so caution must be exercised whenever working with IT. Meanwhile, IT must always strive to understand the intent or vision for the desired future state of a business. That's the only way to determine whether the solution will meet the requirements of a project and its associated scale and complexity. With that appreciation of the larger business vision, then IT can legitimately demand trust in aligning IT strategy with business strategy.

There's a tough word to embrace in IT—vulnerability. Vulnerability in IT generally means weakness, high risk, opportunity to exploit. But I learned in a workshop once that vulnerability is allowing in things that you would never have considered. When I was told in that workshop, "You need to be more vulnerable," I originally thought that meant I needed to be more emotional or weaker—something, as a man, I wasn't immediately willing to do. But I completely missed the mark and eventually did get the message. Being truly vulnerable allows all your defenses to be down so that you can absorb or let in other possibilities. Otherwise, it's like someone who has never tasted broccoli saying, "I hate broccoli."

Part of going beyond basic day-to-day problem-solving is a level of investigation and openness to new ways of more optimally resolving issues, including ways that keep you from repeating the same problem.

GOING HOME

In 2004, I had been working on an EA framework for the Medicaid program, but using a national-level perspective to seek out common aspects of how each state goes about implementing elements of their respective Medicaid program, from concept through operations. It was an attempt to help the states look for opportunities to share best practices and perhaps influence a more holistic approach to finding solutions that could be leveraged more than just once. The work on the MITA framework was noticed by the new CMS chief architect, Debe McKeldin. Debe was taking on the role of the agency's chief architect to reinvigorate the program and to improve the way the agency invested in IT in support of the Medicare program. Debe hired me and brought me over to the Office of Information Services (OIS) to assist her in making the EA program more relevant than it had been. She'd spent most of her career on the policy and operations side of Medicare. That made her the best person for the position, because the theory is that a good EA program and strong IT governance will produce the best business results. To legitimately stand in those shoes and demand change required that the chief architect fully understand the business issues and challenges of the agency, if not the entire health-care industry. Too often, when chief architects are only adept at all things technical, there is limited success in the EA program.

After joining Debe's EA division in OIS, the agency kicked into high gear to finish planning and starting the execution for the implementation of the Medicare Prescription Drug Program—Medicare Part D. The new benefit was a key cornerstone of the Medicare Modernization Act (MMA) that was originally passed in 2003, and by the fall of 2004, the implementation plans were beginning to solidify. The Part D program was slated to begin on January 1, 2006, with open enrollment to begin November 15, 2005. It was anticipated that beneficiary election of the drug benefit, shifting an initial seven million full-benefit dual eligibles (FBDEs, people eligible for both Medicare and Medicaid) from a Medicaid drug benefit to Medicare Part D, and payments of a subsidy to employers to help keep their retirees on their existing drug benefit plans would result in approximately twenty-eight million Part D program beneficiaries in 2006. Since Part D work quickly became the top priority of the agency, I was scooped up by the CTO at the time, Wally Fung. My role was to assist in filling gaps in systems capabilities to fully support the program when operations began as early as summer 2005 and work with states to correctly identify and process FBDEs in preparation for the Part D benefit to kick in for them on January 1, 2006.

Wally was an engineer by training and was steeped in experiences with large-scale systems architectures and building secure, Internet-facing applications. He was a force to be reckoned with, authoritative and authoritarian, but he was the right guy at the right time—there was no one better to ensure that Part D got off the ground. The agency had not undertaken such a major change since it began in 1965, and it needed a hard-nosed, seasoned veteran of complex, large-scale systems implementation and integration experience who wouldn't take guff from anyone. There was no debating the best courses of action with Wally. He was a no-nonsense decision maker who took all the bad with the good and spit out results. Much of what I needed to understand in managing large-scale projects from both technical and business perspectives I learned in a very short time working for Wally and Debe.

When Wally retired in the summer of 2007 with over thirty-five years of federal service, I applied for his position and was selected to be the CTO and appointed to the Senior Executive Service in early 2008. In the wake of Wally's leadership style, the CTO position was modified so that it did not carry as much authority as it had prior. That became a challenge, because I had no staff and no resources. It was the dawn of a new era for the role of CTO. Technically, people didn't have to listen to me—a very precarious position to be in, especially when I needed to get something done. In retrospect, however, it compelled me to be more creative about how to motivate people to do the right thing. The scaled-down authority of the CTO position taught me to be more collaborative and not to rely solely on a title to get things done.

In many ways, the Part D experience was a precursor to taking on the challenges of the ACA Insurance Marketplace program. The scale of operations, complexities, integrations, and need to forge partnerships were similar challenges, as was the need to implement systems and processes that worked in real time to match the real-time eligibility and claims adjudication model of the retail prescription drug industry—a first for the Medicare program. And it wasn't just about planning and implementation, but also how to shift focus from pre–day one to post–day one operations, where it was all about stabilization, emergency system fixes, cleaning up data issues, and supporting casework for people who were adversely impacted by start-up issues.

That included working with congressional staffers in D.C. and in their home district offices to help solve constituency issues with the benefit. It also meant dealing with shifting dual eligible beneficiaries from their Medicaid-sponsored prescription drug plans to Medicare Part D plans—all while being summoned to twelve-hour depositions over various lawsuits against the federal government.

While implementing programs such as Part D, patterns developed. They included working with the best available information, which sometimes is far from perfect information, executing the work within a fixed timeframe, and dynamically adapting to ever-changing circumstances, then stepping back, considering the lessons learned, and applying those lessons to the next round of challenges. Recognizing that cycle further enhanced the ability to rapidly adapt to very difficult situations and still be able to make some degree of forward progress without being paralyzed by a bad situation where there are no clear or good options.

In the twenty-one years I worked at HCFA, then CMS, every administration wanted to do something to "transform" health care. Typically, that meant targeting Medicare and/or Medicaid, because both have the largest pools of enrollment with over fifteen million people that are dually eligible in both Medicare and Medicaid. Medicare alone presently has over fifty-five million beneficiaries, and its policies and models of access and delivery influence every insurance company and provider organization in the country. Changes to Medicare generally create a ripple effect throughout the health-care industry.

By 2008, when President Obama began his first term, there was again the prospect of transforming health care. Taking on a challenge of increasing access to affordable care for at least a large portion of the fifty-four million uninsured back in 2008 and 2009 was the charge.

As policies were being formulated and politics were going through the processes between the Hill and the White House, many of us in CMS and HHS, due to our experience in bringing up Part D, were asked to examine draft pieces of potential legislation and formulate possible high-level solutions and costs for two proposed models—the public option from the House and the state-based exchange from the Senate.

Even though I was not privy to complete portions of the proposed legislative text, the pieces I reviewed and contemplated solutions for allowed me early preview into some of the complexities of implementing the ACA, whichever option was ultimately passed.

All the way up to Christmas 2009, there was a lot of cajoling in the House and Senate over various elements of each version of the bill. When Congress went on Christmas recess, it looked like all was lost—the ACA was not going to happen. But after the session convened in January, Nancy Pelosi, House Speaker at the time, managed to get the House to vote on the Senate version of the bill and went to the president for signature. While that was a shrewd move, it meant that the bill signed into law did not have the usual reconciliation between the House and Senate versions, which may have had greater bipartisan support. Nonetheless, President Obama signed the ACA into law in March 2010.

Shortly after the passage of the ACA, the OCIIO was formed and charged with implementing the key sections of the ACA dealing with insurance reform, consumer protections, and the centerpiece— the Insurance Marketplace. In my role as CTO of CMS, I continued to work almost daily with the initial OCIIO team that was formed with many familiar people from around HHS until around June, when discussions began with IRS and planning kicked into high gear. During a working session one day, I threw up my hands and said, half-jokingly, "I'm basically working for you guys, so I might as well join you." At the time, there was a "no poaching" rule created around people who were dedicated to the ACA as opposed to being on loan, which meant that people could not be solicited from other agencies to work for the OCIIO unless they voluntarily inquired about joining on a more permanent basis. Since I had opened the door, I was welcomed to join the organization to help build what I had already been working on.

In July 2010, I officially left CMS and moved over to become CIO of OCIIO, to lead the effort to build an IT organization and to start planning and coordination for what technical capabilities were needed to support OCIIO's mission. We kickstarted a funding opportunity announcement to attract states that were motivated to set up their own exchanges to come in for what was called the "Early Innovator State" grant program to try and get at least a few states engaged and thinking about a potential accelerated path toward implementation.

MOST OF OUR EFFORTS WERE DESIGNED TO SAVE TIME AND MANAGE THE RISK OF NOT HAVING ENOUGH TIME AND RESOURCES.

We shared high-level requirements that were developed, but it was still too early in the process in the fall of 2010 to have any significant details of the policies. Thus, any details for requirements beyond high-level notional architectures and business process models were still lacking. I and many of my seasoned colleagues could already tell that progress on policy details would be a long and difficult road given the magnitude of the changes involved in how health insurance was purchased in 2010 versus the expected future model of online enrollment by 2013. Hence, most of our efforts were designed to save time and manage the risk of not having enough time and resources.

Seven months after the passage of ACA, we could already see how risky it was going to be. Add to the mix of issues the 2010 midterm elections, when the Republicans won back the majority in the House. By January 2011, HHS and the administration decided to move the OCIIO organization to CMS, renaming it the Center for Consumer Information & Insurance Oversight (CCIIO). The CCIIO needed an "older sibling" to help stand it up and grow its base of experience in developing and implementing public policy programs and carrying those forward to ever-so-carefully improve and optimize its service delivery to the public.

I wasn't surprised by the move given what I witnessed between July and December 2010—the political turmoil, the lack of focus around which priorities to work on, indecision on the scarce finances, poor support for hiring, lack of experienced leadership in this politically intense area—all of which added to the already daunting task of reshaping how health insurance is sold and purchased in the United States. Mostly what I saw at that time was an overall lack of realism regarding the time that was needed for the tasks at hand.

After witnessing that turmoil, any reasonable person would have ran in the other direction, but that wasn't my reaction. Instead, I felt an ever-growing, deeper commitment to make the program work.

Moving to CMS in one respect felt like going home. However, I knew that when organizations merge, the tendency is for the bigger and more mature organization to make the newer, smaller organization operate more like itself. But there's inevitably resistance, particularly when the sentiment turns negative about the new organization bringing its unwanted baggage. The next thing you know, you're sleeping in the basement.

In theory, such a move might have been beneficial for some areas of operations such as contracting, budget, and HR, but in reality, these became just more needy components inside a larger organization already contending with resource and bandwidth issues. That was particularly true in the efforts to continue building up and staffing the IT organization meant to support the Insurance Marketplace program.

There are stark differences between being in CMS and being in the IRS. In June 2010, during an initial kickoff meeting between HHS and IRS, I sat across a long conference table from Terry Milholland, the CTO of IRS. From the minute I met Terry, I could tell he was a great person to work with and had a great sense of humor. He asked how our hiring efforts were going.

"Slowly," I replied.

Then he asked how many IT staff were on board.

I looked around at Monique Outerbridge, my dependable deputy, and Mike Lorsbach, my trustworthy special assistant, then said to Terry, "Counting the two behind me makes a total of three."

Terry smiled but laughed nervously.

"Why," I countered, "how many staff do you have?"

"Seven thousand," he replied.

Over the next three years, until around mid-2013, the IRS added another four hundred staff to work on its pieces of the ACA. Meanwhile, my IT group in CMS ballooned to a whopping fifty-five staff.

The staff equation was lopsided for many reasons, but the most difficult to explain is why CMS, which was responsible for the systems that needed to perform online enrollment by the earlier date of October 1, 2013, wasn't weighted like the IRS's piece, which was to reconcile advance premium tax credits (APTCs) beginning in the tax filing period for 2014, which was actually in 2015.

In retrospect, if we had not moved to CMS, the House Republicans would have had a field day targeting us like sitting ducks as part of the Office of the Secretary of HHS. At the time, it looked like the best decision to make the best of the new political realities, but there were downsides.

CMS is a large organization, with most of its resources devoted to administering and operating the Medicare program. CMS is organized around centers and offices. Centers are the primary drivers of policy and business matters in Medicare, Medicaid, CHIP, ACA Payment and Delivery System Reforms, and the ACA Insurance Marketplaces. Over 130 million lives are touched by CMS programs, and its programs are the core engines of how health care is financed, accessed, and delivered. Its annual program outlays, including the costs of operating the agency and programs, exceed $1.3 trillion. It might seem the CMS would have tens of thousands of employees around the country, but in fact, there are only about six thousand employees. CMS's lineage traces back to the SSA after the passage of Medicare and Medicaid, Title 18 and 19 respectively, which were amendments to the original Social Security Act. In the early 1970s, HCFA was established, and since more beneficiaries were in the program, more health-care providers were participating, leading to growth in the volume of health-care services and claims called for establishing an agency to oversee this growth and to create efficiencies and automation in the programs. When HCFA transitioned into CMS, there was no other health insurance payer in the world that processed as many claims, enrollments, and health-care data as CMS. On its face, moving OCIIO to CMS was a prudent move, but in reality, it was a move to ensure that the work of OCIIO could continue in driving the centerpiece of the ACA—the Insurance Marketplace.

CMS has multiple funding streams and broad, deep experience in the fundamentals of operating and administering highly visible and politicized health-care programs that are the largest in the world. Those fundamentals include managing budgets, contracting and procurements, grants, developing legislation into policies and regulations, managing and coordinating with other parts of the executive and legislative branches, coordinating and performing oversight and rendering federal guidance to state and local governments, managing the labyrinth of clearance processes for polices and regulations, enterprise approaches to building and maintaining IT systems at a national scale, political savvy in managing internal and external communications with the public, and understanding the tremendous differences between what it takes to launch a national program and what it takes to operationally sustain it for years and decades.

One of the significant downsides of being back with the CMS was its established culture, which had great difficulty embracing and adapting to a new portfolio of work that significantly threatened the already strained resources of not only its day-to-day operations, but also its priorities for what it needed to implement—the significant changes specified in ACA for Medicare. Too much time was expended in multiple parallel attempts to bring budgeting, contracting, and hiring the right people in harmony rather than retaining the dedicated support OCIIO had before it came to CMS. The staff working on those areas were "farmed out" to CMS including the IT group that I established. (Later, in 2015, the CCIIO decided to reclaim the former dedicated IT group to its programs and moved it from the Office of Information Technology back to the Center for Consumer Information and Insurance Insight.) The staff was then absorbed into the respective CMS components while all of the policy people and teams remained in place to staff the CCIIO and the Center for Medicare and Medicaid Innovation (CMMI), which was also created by ACA.

CHAPTER 2

THE US HEALTH CARE SYSTEM—IT'S COMPLICATED

The health-care system in the United States before the ACA represents a patchwork of efforts spanning multiple decades to provide health-care coverage for targeted groups such as the poor, elderly, disabled, veterans, employees, and many other groups. However, there was nothing that created a simple set of eligibility rules that basically opened the door for all. With so many sets of eligibility rules and with some that required coordination of one or more types of eligibility is at the root of most of the complexity. Think of the possible cost savings that would come from eliminating these multiple pathways to coverage and all the administrative costs to manage these rules program by program, each with a massive investments to operate and maintain the systems and operations just for the eligibility portion of the health-care process. It would not be a trivial sum, and can be then applied to offset the costs of treating people rather than spending a large portion of each dollar for the administration of all these rules and disparate processes. But unfortunately, this is the complicated world of health care in which we all have to navigate. That patchwork of programs and access options includes employment with a large company or small business, transition-in-life situations such as COBRA, lack of means to personally acquire coverage, public policy initiatives intended to improve people's lives, disability status, student status, temporary status for occupational injuries or automobile-related injuries, military status, veteran status, retiree status, membership in an organization, special programs focused on specific illnesses and/or age groups, public health initiatives, and self-pay individuals purchasing health-care coverage.

Add up all the people covered under these and there are still more than fifty million people without coverage. A small portion of that number are people who, for one reason or another, do not want health-care coverage and/or are of sufficient means to self-pay and not have to apply and be evaluated for eligibility in order to get coverage. A fairly large portion of people in that number have been denied coverage because of some preexisting condition. Then there are some who just roll the dice and go along without coverage.

Some politicians grossly oversimplify the issue by saying everyone has coverage because they can always go to the emergency room for care. There are a couple of short sells with that ideology. One is that when health-care providers such as hospitals incur a significant amount of unpaid services, that liability is then shifted to Medicare and/or Medicaid, so then everyone pays. The other short sell is that not every treatment begins and ends in the ER. What happens when the diagnosis is a critical condition requiring constant care or high-cost medications? Although it's easy to agree with the politicians that an ER can always provide care, it's dangerous to oversimplify this particular issue. Who wouldn't have a dramatic change of heart after being diagnosed with a chronic illness or deadly disease—or having a family or friend in such a position—and having no coverage to pay for it? When health care becomes highly personal, speculation quickly changes into something real and dire. That is the tipping point in the debate about whether health care is a right or a privilege. Parents caring for chronically ill children would never, ever debate about rights and privileges of access to health care. Why would anyone not be able to see that point? My guess is that the people who stand on the wrong side of that debate are people who have always had health-care coverage, such as members of Congress and all of their staff. The objectives of ACA were to decrease the cost of health care in the United States, improve its quality, and make it more accessible, particularly for the uninsured.

The details behind the goals were intricate and intended to lay the groundwork for health insurance reform and address the transformation that was needed after decades of repeated debates about who drives the change and where to shift the costs in a third-party payer system. Many people in the United States, including some members of Congress and their staff, do not realize how health-care costs are distributed across the spectrum of stakeholders, participants, and influencers of our health-care system. Whenever someone is being treated in a health-care setting, particularly in higher-cost settings such as hospitals and skilled nursing homes, the total costs of all the care provided is covered through a complex web of eligibility, coverage, and reimbursement formulas, sometimes shared by multiple payers. An example is someone who has employer retiree coverage, is also over sixty-five and Medicare eligible, and has Veteran's Administration (VA) coverage because of a service-connected disability.

One of the key lessons I learned early on in my career working, mostly on the federal side of the Medicaid program, is that the complexities of technologies used in small- or large-scale designs of systems stem from the fact that people do not live static lives. And these systems have to keep up with processing information that track with the dynamically changing aspects of one's life changing events that affect eligibility. Youth under eighteen may have health-care coverage from their parents or a foster care program. They might attend college and be covered by health insurance sponsored by the academic institution. They might join the military. People get married, have children, adopt children, get divorced, remarry, change jobs, have fluctuating income levels, move every few years, and have changing health conditions. It takes numerous systems to keep up with these changes in order to properly assess and, to the greatest degree possible, accurately process the information. Yet, those systems are limited by the constraints of how information is allowed to flow in government systems that have to abide by much more stringent security and privacy rules compared to most commercial businesses. At the same time, people want their government to be conservative in how it works with the public's information and when and how information is shared, unlike the social media model where the default setting is share everything, although as of recent days, Facebook and other social media sites are all revising their privacy and data use policies. All of these factors must be considered when determining the starting point in how much change can realistically be attained in an increment of time.

Many people swooped in after October 1, 2013 and provided their opinions and assessment of what went wrong during the HealthCare.gov rollout. The irony was that the vast majority of opinions and speculations about the rollout were incorrect in their most basic assumptions of the origin or root causes behind it. Simply put: the rollout happened the way it did because it had to in order to draw enough attention and convince people to examine what we were actually trying to accomplish in a relatively short time. In situations like this, we all need to exercise a little caution in not hastily rendering judgement without a fairly accurate picture of what is really happening and what actually contributed to the situation.

The amount of change the ACA was attempting to make in an already imperfect health-care system was all conceptual until it actually had to happen in the manner proposed. It added to an already complicated system a set of requirements that would further complicate how health-care coverage was going to be "accessible." Those requirements included online, real-time enrollments and adjudication of a range of eligibility categories integrating Insurance Marketplace rules with states that expanded Medicaid and states that chose not to expand Medicaid. And all of it had to be a "world-class experience."

When we say something is complicated, such as in the way our health-care system functions, the comment doesn't necessarily mean it's negative or even positive in itself. When we hear something is complicated, we should make an attempt at understanding why the complexity exists rather than writing it off as something that doesn't deserve the attention it ought to have. This is absolutely necessary to be an effective problem solver. Anyone can point out a negative or create emphasis on the negative, but it takes real effort to understand and deal with the complex in order to progressively move toward solving the problem, Granted, there's neither legislation nor anything proposed to simplify what is happening in the health-care world. But if we don't try to understand that complexity, we are doomed to make less-informed decisions and will have to accept the trappings until we decide to understand what we have so we don't keep reinventing infinite versions of the same complexities.

Indeed, health care is complex. Now think about what is involved in designing and building systems that follow that complexity, then ratchet that up to a national level and use technology to automate and create efficiencies.

Still, although a challenge, the intent of ACA was and still is a good one. It was a major, but necessary disruptive event in health care to benefit people who need health-care coverage that sufficiently meets their needs, whether they know it or not. Regardless of the politics, it was a noble endeavor, a starting line for change. No matter all the challenges of planning, training, and preparation, no matter what went right or wrong—as of October 1, 2013, it launched.

Of the more than 270 million people in 2013 who had some form of health-care coverage, how many truly understood how health insurance (employer, public, private) worked in the United States? How many stakeholders were involved who had a say in the care received? The number is much, much lower than the 270 million.

From a consumer perspective, spending the better part of forty-two months (the time between passage of ACA and the launch of HealthCare.gov) developing the policies and rules for the coverage, benefits, subsidies, and access to affordable health insurance to fundamentally change how the individual and small group health insurance markets operated meant two things: first, a change to the rules for guaranteed issuance or can't-be-denied-coverage for preexisting conditions, and second, the ability to enroll online and get real-time information on coverage and monthly premiums. The accelerated model that guaranteed coverage for anyone who applied sped up the process to get health-care coverage. But there was still the challenge of how to best understand the details of that coverage.

Just ask yourself about your own coverage and your children, parents, siblings, etc. Would you know precisely the dynamics of the relationships between deductibles, co-insurance, co-pays, out-of-pocket limits, catastrophic caps, cost-sharing formulas, and the monthly/annual premiums paid by you and/or your employer or government-sponsored coverage? How many people actually fully grasp the true cost of health care and the basis for comparison? What contributes to the lack of understanding on one hand is certainly the opaqueness of the US health-care system with regard to the coverage benefits and overall cost. On the other hand, it's the lack of understanding of how the costs are calculated and derived—whether by region of the country, demographics of the populations, age, smoking status, gender, health status, etc. The ACA provided for greater transparency and understanding of coverage benefits to give consumers a better chance of comparing "apples to apples" across heath plan products that offered the same benefits while varying in price to compete for business.

The ACA revived a long-standing debate about whether health care is a right or a privilege. In the age of low tolerance for facts and even less awareness of the history behind such a debate, there's less than zero probability that you'll have a change of heart and position by simply putting yourself in the shoes of a parent trying to care for a sick child. I think most people who want to debate this from a pure economics and social policy perspective forget that health care in the US is a business, and by design, businesses are supposed to be profitable and the drive to produce ever growing revenue is the backdrop of how much of what we experience when we engage in the health-care system. Hospitals and physicians can't possibly be successful at treating people if they themselves can't pay their bills and meet their payroll. Insurance companies won't survive on paying claims and not increasing premiums and/or decreasing their risk exposure. So wrapped up in the heated debate is the ACA individual mandate. Imposing an individual mandate to all that are qualified to enroll in health-care coverage must do so or be subject to a modest penalty. This is not a right or privilege discussion, it's an apparatus to increase the insurance risk pools to help balance out a revised equation that includes quite a bit of upside for tens of millions of people. The ACA also brought about guaranteed issuance so that people would not be denied coverage for preexisting conditions. Again, for anyone who has experienced a situation where a loved one's health issues caused economic hardship or forced a discussion about being able to afford the proper care, the debate about having health-care coverage as a privilege or right becomes a non-starter. Those on the side of calling it a privilege—meaning that it is a person's own responsibility to ensure that they can pay for all the costs of health care—have likely never been in a health crisis themselves or with a family member, where all they should be worrying about is the patient getting better but instead have to always be considering the costs involved.

I've personally heard congressional people say that children can always rely on the charity of Shriner's Hospital or St. Jude's—organizations that cover the costs for families that need adequate care for their child. What sensible and moral person would say such a thing—let alone an elected official using that as a reason not to worry about health-care coverage? Again, it's all academics when it's a faceless person or group, until it becomes your own personal reality—a child or loved one who needs care that is out of reach because of its cost.

While the ACA won't ever solve the debate, it moves us closer to becoming a society that is overt about its public policies on health care, if not for all, then for as many as possible.

Contrast the debate over health care in the United States with a universal health-care system, such as those in the United Kingdom or Canada. In that model, everyone is eligible for health care. In the US system, other than a dire emergency, before you can be seen by a health-care provider, your eligibility and coverage type has to be verified at least once in your initial encounter. Once eligibility is confirmed, then the next hurdle is to get people enrolled in coverage. It doesn't mean reinventing the entire health-care system, but it means looking at the current health-care system to see how to leverage the existing access and delivery methods to expand coverage, which in part, is what ACA is trying to do—some positive level of disruption with minimal endangerment to what coverages existed.

Donald Trump said, "Nobody knew health care could be so complicated." While a sad reflection of the world's most powerful leader, his statement encompasses the challenge of explaining and getting through to people what really is an improvement to the US health-care system when you're not quite sure how it even works, or whether any one improvement benefits or harms individuals, various categories of the population, health-care practitioners, and/or the health-care industry. His statement is illustrative of a very wide swath of people in this country who find trying to navigate the health-care system to be a real mystery. But that doesn't mean anyone can let themselves off the hook—throwing up your hands and complaining that it's too complicated perpetuates the mystery factor. Implementing major improvements to the US health-care system requires enough recognition and acceptance that the status quo isn't working to improve the health and economic welfare of this country.

When something that's big and extremely complicated needs to undergo change, it's going to be somewhat messy. Before it can even be evaluated as good or bad, it must first be recognized that it's enormously complicated. And the knowledge of those complexities helps provide the ability to project what could possibly work in a short amount of time. A lot of what I encountered was people who raised questions based only on their varying levels of understanding of their one little slice of the whole problem.

Anytime you're trying to get a sense of just how big a program such as ACA is, it's easy to look at the money spent, the number of people enrolled, number of states involved, number of insurers, number of health plan products, and who the key stakeholders groups are that are involved. Those statistics are out there. In fact, with regard to macro, national level statistics with regard to Medicare and Medicaid programs, CMS prints a fact book from the actuary's office every year that contains all the volumes and metrics associated with the programs.

IMPLEMENTING MAJOR IMPROVEMENTS TO THE US HEALTH CARE SYSTEM REQUIRES ENOUGH RECOGNITION AND ACCEPTANCE THAT THE STATUS QUO ISN'T WORKING TO IMPROVE THE HEALTH AND ECONOMIC WELFARE OF THIS COUNTRY.

Because of all the policies and business rules involved, health insurance is far more complex than insurance for a house, an auto, a person (life insurance), or perhaps harder to understand. Because with other insurance other than health insurance, there's greater familiarity in terms of coverage, premiums, deductibles, etc., as compared to the pre-ACA days of high variability across states, insurers, and health plan products thus making it quite difficult to pin down the exact basket of goods you are getting with any given type of health insurance simply because not all products were created equal. And health insurance must look at how to cover not only individuals but also accommodate a household that may be comprised of people with varying circumstances and attributes that contribute towards determining eligibility for coverage.

So developing policies and business rules for determining eligibility, then implementing the rules as part of an online application process that checks federal authoritative data sources, and finally coordinating business rules with state Medicaid and CHIP programs was a massive undertaking when implementing ACA. Other points of coordination within the eligibility determination process also needed to be aware of anyone on the application that may already have access to minimum essential coverage such as through Federal Employee Health Benefits (FEHB), Veteran Affairs, Tricare, Peace Corps, Medicaid, CHIP, and Medicare.

All of these processes must be well understood before even arriving at the point of building or changing a system or adding more features and capabilities. In the case of the Insurance Marketplace, new eligibility rules had to be built to efficiently coordinate with what rules already were in place in existing systems. Plus, there were integration and coordination factors to consider, because none of the programs started and stayed in a vacuum. The health care needs of most people often change as people experience life changing events such as marriage, birth of a child, adoption of a child, fostering a child, divorce, change in employment status, moving from state to state, and more, which means that as you translate new program requirements into design such as an online enrollment experience, you must consider the dynamic nature in which people live their lives. And at the point in which people engage a process such as enrolling in health-care coverage online, you must also consider that the information you collect and process represent information that is temporal and could represent only a snapshot in time and not something that can be presumed to be constant and not subject to change. Just consider your own experience in going through life changing events you've had in the last ten years or even longer, and the numerous status changes you needed to provide insurance companies, employers, state and federal government agencies, and financial institutions so that your information and records are kept up-to-date.

PEOPLE LEAD MESSY LIVES

Quite frankly, systems that support health-care administration, access, delivery, and payment are complicated largely due to the dynamic nature of how people live their lives. Health insurance programs and their associated systems are constantly trying to keep up with each individual's life-changing circumstances.

Just think for a minute about all the information initially, and on an ongoing basis, that you have to provide to your insurer. All of that information is collected, processed, and used to determine your initial and ongoing eligibility. Then eligibility rules are applied based on information such as age, marital status, income level, working status, and other factors of your life. All of those rules were based on policies and business requirements that had to be in place in the system to appropriately process your information when you first applied for coverage and subsequent changes that occurred in your life.

Imagine how challenging it is to track all of those life-changing circumstances across a span of time or your entire lifetime and to have the correct status at any one point in time. For example, the Social Security Administration tracks people from birth to death and some of the most critical functions they perform for the public is to work with people who are applying for retirement benefits, disability, and to help shepherd people who have become eligible for Medicare. The critical information SSA collects, tracks, processes, and shares with other agencies, such as CMS, is a tremendously large-scale and complex operation in which health-care programs like Medicare greatly depend on.

So, people lead messy lives, and in order for people's information in health-care systems to be as accurate as possible, all the inputs flowing from initial engagement to ongoing changes, including information flowing from government authoritative sources such as SSA's Death Master File, must be tracked in the health-care system to determine eligibility—who's in, who's out, and for what reason.

Since the very early days of mocking up wireframes for Health-Care.gov and thinking in earnest about how to best shepherd an applicant through the process of online enrollment for themselves and potentially an entire household, we had to consider all the possible permutations of how people dynamically live their lives and how to best capture point-in-time information as well as providing the ability to return and update information on any life changing circumstances. Perhaps you could say that we were trying to provide for a world-class experience, but more importantly was factoring the entire range of possible circumstances in which an applicant would need accommodated in their initial enrollment plus accommodations for what may change going forward.

THE PROCESS

The risks involved in implementing programs such as the ACA can increase due to established government processes in which you have no direct control over. When government undertakes a direction or a policy that's set forth by the legislative or executive branch, it must go through a structured process designed to be highly inclusive of the public in what it does. For example, if a law is passed, the law really serves as the high-level framework for the ideals, outcomes, and ways that policy is to be financed by the government. It frames that set of public policy intent.

The next step in the journey is the rule-making, or regulation, process. The regulations are not detailed guidance, but they spell out how programs will operate, how the funding mechanisms will work, the types of data that will be collected, and the impact to the economy of a given sector or sectors that the law and regulation would impact. In the case of health care, there would be an impact on costs, coverage, and the number of people covered, so that impact analysis is also included.

Then there's a public comment period where the regulation is published in the federal register for a number of days, generally sixty days or so. The "public" in "public comment" is a very broad term. Individuals can certainly submit comments on the regulation back to the government, but most commenters on regulations in the health-care sector are representing groups of interested parties such as the American Medical Association, American Hospital Association, and other industry associations that represent insurers, health IT vendors, and many others that have a stake in any major change to the US health-care landscape.

Then all the comments are factored into the final regulation. That final regulation is published and stands as the next level of detail in the framework for implementation.

Concurrently, as the proposed regulation moves through the process to final regulation, agencies were already assigned responsibility not just for writing the regulation and shepherding it through the process, but also responsibility for implementation, as was the case with HHS and CMS, start looking at the implications of bringing up that program. That includes everything from organizational structure and human resources to budget and contracting.

Typically, throughout the rule-making process, the policies begin to mature and are vetted through the public comment process and further details emerge in the form of sub-regulatory guidance such as formal letters to certain official bodies, bulletins, briefings, etc. Through multiple iterations driving to greater details about the program and policies including sometimes taking a step backwards to regroup and realign, we document business requirements and other associated artifacts that are necessary for design and development of the system or systems. In theory, as the process unfolds, you eventually have enough clear requirements identified for all the stakeholders involved to make progress towards implementation. Typically, there's never enough time to work out every last detail by the first implementation date, but in the case of how the ACA unfolded from passage of the law to regulation to requirements the process had to withstand numerous other constraints brought about by tremendous political opposition to the implementation of the law. What usually is already a frantic pace to get as much done as possible in the allotted time under normal circumstances, became significantly more challenging to conduct the process from law to implementation with great clarity and transparency under ACA.

THE SECURITY OF THE DATA

In some cases, the process can take place in less than a year. In other cases, it can take multiple years. It's understandably bureaucratic—after all, you don't want your government to make unilateral decisions about what data it collects and shares about citizens. That's why there are laws and regulations such as the Health Insurance Portability and Accountability Act (HIPAA) to govern how the government or other entities handle your data and keep it secure and how they work with you to understand the allowable uses and your preferences for sharing that data.

In that context, people begin to understand that they want the government to provide benefits and services as it should, as dictated by Congress and the executive branch, but at the same time, they want caution exercised in the secure design and implementation of the program that provides those services. For example, most people do not want a program that creates unsecure situations with the collection and handling of their data.

Within health care, there is an abundance of caution along with a duty and responsibility to ensure that no information is shared unless there is a specific, sanctioned use of that data set by precedence, by a regulation, or by law. Again, the system is understandably bureaucratic because people generally want their government to be very cautious about how it handles their information and how it operates the programs that are supposed to help people, such as facilitating health-care coverage.

THE MONEY FLOW—FROM THE FEDS AND THE STATES

Of the federal, state, and local governments, the federal government has the greatest taxing authority, and, in our federalist system, it is generally looked upon by states as a good *and* evil twin. The good that it provides is that it generally can, through national economic and tax policies, generate revenue for the government at much greater volumes than each individual state. Thus, it can help states implement and operate programs such as Medicaid. The states, in many cases, tolerate the federal government because Big Brother has a pretty large purse.

The downside is that the purse comes with rules and regulations about how the money is used. The tension in that relationship exists in part because states have to work individually and collectively to establish their aspect of public policy implementation. In the case of the ACA largely passed in the form of the Senate version of the legislation, the expected model was that states would set up their own respective state-based marketplace (SBM) using very generous federal grant dollars rather than opting out of building their own and deferring to the federal government to provide for the functionality through the federally facilitated marketplace (FFM).

Then there's also the fact that very large states like California, Texas, and New York have numerous counties, some of which are larger than some states. For instance, Los Angeles County in California is larger than the state of Rhode Island. County-based services, such as the social services offered locally, in many cases serve as the frontlines in managing health and human services programs. This is an important factor to consider because through much of the pathways that existed just prior to ACA, and even after in many cases, consumers find their way to healthcare coverage through their overall interaction with various channels that assist people in identifying a range of benefits they might be eligible for, from food and nutrition assistance to housing assistance to medical assistance. In this case, the ACA context can mean eventual enrollment in the Medicaid program in a given state or perhaps the children in that same household enrolled in the state's CHIP program, or some in the household may even be determined to qualify to enroll in an Insurance Marketplace plan with or without premium assistance. What existed in the context of how people found their way to health-care coverage prior to ACA had to be factored in to how the enrollment process would work for Insurance Marketplaces because the new ACA requirements involved a significant amount of business process, system, and data/information integration in order to produce a good or perhaps even a "world-class experience" for the consumer that has to navigate through a meld of the old and new.

Therefore, complex technological challenges begin with complex business and policy changes. Rarely, if ever, are new programs fully thought through in an operational context that must make sense of what is brought up as new that then has to coexist with what already is in the ecosystem. One of the most valuable experiences while at CMS was being directly exposed to, and being responsible for, large-scale complex systems integrations where new program requirements expose all the less than optimal "short-term" solutions that now exist as limitations or constraints to what you are trying to achieve with the new program, such as being able to enroll people in health-care coverage and adjudication their application while online and in real-time. The valuable experience isn't just being exposed to that challenge, but also being able to find solutions that can properly service the new requirements while not endangering and gravely disrupting existing critical processes.

TACKLING PIECES INSTEAD OF THE WHOLE

Projects the size and scope of the ACA are about more than just traversing technical issues. They involve first learning about the programs and policies, and the interconnections and dependencies inherent in the US health-care system. I was attracted to those complexities, having already encountered several large-scale CMS challenges and relishing the sense of ownership in handling all that they presented. But in overseeing the transformation that became HealthCare.gov, a number of new lessons were learned—lessons that I believe can be useful when overseeing a big project in either the public or private sector. In the following chapters, I will share these lessons in hopes that they help others facing similar challenges.

CHAPTER 3

NEVER STOP LEARNING

In July 2010, we started to ramp up hiring efforts to recruit staff who were experienced in IT architecture, project management, systems analysis, requirements management, IT budget and contracting, and information security. The hiring process was a bit slow due to uncertainties with the overall ACA budget shortages, but we managed to bring in about a dozen or so staff by the fall of 2010. In an ideal situation, since the office was created eight months prior, we should have had at least three to four divisions staffed out with additional support staff dedicated to myself and my deputy, Monique Outerbridge.

Even though the number of IT staff was small, I wanted to get an early start in helping them grasp just how large and complex it would be and to focus on incremental progress toward a deadline in which they all had to constantly remind the people they work with that the start of the program would be rough and that not everything everyone wants will be available on day one.

Every other week or so during staff meetings, I would take time to conduct some information sharing and informal training to help staff properly frame the challenges at hand. Much of what was needed to optimally perform duties in such a politically toxic environment as the HealthCare.gov rollout did not involve having stupendous technical skills. While technical skills were important, the organizational and cultural differences, highly volatile and undependable budget, extremely erratic decision-making processes on policies, and the need to make progress with the best available information required a philosophy for embracing whatever came along while staying focused on delivering the minimum viable product (MVP). Without the proper framing, stamina, and belief that we could persevere, no amount of technical skills would result in the actual delivery of a viable product.

THE FIRST STEP, I EXPLAINED, WAS TO ADMIT THERE IS SOMETHING THAT THEY KNOW THEY DON'T KNOW. FROM THERE, THEY MUST ACTUALLY LEARN WHAT THEY DON'T KNOW AND INCREASE THEIR ABILITY TO SEE WHAT MAY BE POSSIBLE.

One of the understandings I wanted the team to have was about properly framing the amount of knowledge that everyone brings to the table based on their previous experiences. To demonstrate the point I wanted to make, I used something I learned in a workshop that opened my eyes as to how I approached problem-solving. I drew a circle representing a pie graph on chart paper with the total area allocated in two quarters and one half of the pie. One quarter of the pie, I explained, represented the sum total of what we already knew. Then I referred to the other quarter and explained that it represented all the things that we know we don't know. For example, I know that I don't know how to fly a plane. The remaining half of the pie, I explained, represented all the knowledge that we don't know we don't know. The first step to take once you understand this illustration is to recalibrate how you approach solving problems. If you are not aware, or not even willing to concede that there are things for which you don't know other possibilities exist, then how do you make informed decisions? I would ask the staff to consider how to shrink that half of the pie, starting with, at minimum, discovering other possibilities to factor into their problem-solving approach. The first step, I explained, was to admit there is something that they know they don't know. From there, they must actually learn what they don't know and increase their ability to see what may be possible.

One of the key aspects of being effective in IT is to adopt the know/don't know approach toward learning, particularly outside the technical domain, and to learn the business domain. Don't be too comfortable in your presently defined universe of knowledge and understanding, because that may trick you into thinking you are already equipped with everything you need for solving problems that you have not yet even seen, let alone comprehend. In my observation, so many people in the IT domain

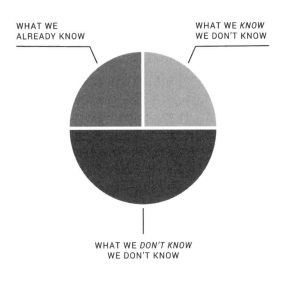

PIE CHART OF PROBLEM-SOLVING

WHAT WE
ALREADY KNOW

WHAT WE *KNOW*
WE DON'T KNOW

WHAT WE *DON'T KNOW*
WE DON'T KNOW

leap to conclusions before they fully understand the problem, and to correctly address that issue is to first help people redefine what they may not be fully encompassing in terms of possible, workable answers.

EMBRACE THE IDEA OF A BETTER WAY

There are many ways to solve problems differently by just slowing down and listening to what the problem is. That applies across the board, regardless of whether you are part of the disciplines of technology (design, development, etc.) or business/policy (health policy, public policy, public health, etc.), or any other discipline. If you either choose not to see or can't imagine the possibilities in which you could create a better way to do something on behalf of the people you serve or the partners that you rely on to better serve the public, what you are really unconsciously doing is steering by your own preferences for the status quo because you aren't even aware of the possibilities of a better way.

It's difficult to confront this challenge of considering a better way to get something done. Often the first reaction is to question why anyone would do something different than it has always been done before, especially if you have been part of previous successful endeavors using the same approach such as choosing a particular type and brand of technology. When you don't consider that the new problem you are given to solve could potentially require a different approach, it is likely you will defer to what has been done in the past and that can contribute to incurring more risk than choosing an approach that is not as common as most people in IT are accustomed to. For every type and brand of technology that exists you will find both supporters and opposers. The key things to remember are to listen closely to what the problem is and to choose an approach and solution that best fits the situation rather than what may be comfortable and familiar to you. Another trapping not to fall into is confusing passion with the need to be right. Clearly, you have to take a stand when you know that a particular approach is better suited for a given situation but try to present it so that it's not about you being right. Typically, when it's detected that it's a battle of will rather than a discussion about what is best suited for a given situation, it then brings out all the heated passions of what each believes is right. When people perceive that you are someone who always has to be right, that in itself is enough to create significant opposition.

When working on complex and large-scale change that affects millions of people, thousands of insurance products, and dozens of government programs and their sponsoring agencies—change that also includes taking on the challenge of overcoming the accumulated technical debt and institutionalized inefficiencies—everyone working on the project/initiative should consider that there are better and sometimes more appropriate ways to make progress against a tight schedule and get things done. New challenges deserve consideration that different solutions may exist. Even if the new challenges share similarities with previous ones, it shouldn't be assumed that whatever was done in the past will work for this new situation. What can be equally as detrimental is leaping to the conclusion to use the newest shiny toys on the tech trend buzz train can be equally problematic. A good and realistic example is rushing to migrate or build systems in the Cloud for no other reason than a belief that it's always better to be in a Cloud.

While there were (and still are) significant challenges with the Insurance Marketplace program, two of the worst were gross over-simplification and lack of recognition of the complexities. These consistently and unnecessarily encumbered the ability to make progress toward determining the necessary requirements to design and build the systems needed by a program that completely challenged the status quo in how health insurance products are brought to markets, how consumers interact online to purchase the products with no possibility of denial for preexisting conditions, and the roles of the federal and state government agencies that are intertwined throughout the product life cycle.

It was a massive endeavor to reengineer business processes that existed and to create new business processes that were driven by an online, real-time model for determining eligibility status, product selection, calculation of subsidies, and application of these to offset premium costs, ultimately resulting in an online enrollment confirmation. All the discussions of the role that technology played in the rollout erroneously shifts the focus toward looking for answers from the tech side. The more productive way to understand what happened and hopefully avoid similar situations in the future would be to include both the business and technical challenges in a discussion about exactly what could have gone better in the effort to plan and implement HealthCare.gov.

Gross oversimplification of the challenges at hand back in 2010 led to two realities. One reality was the irregular and erratic pace at which people moved in determining how best to publicly share the policies, regulations, and overall guidance to stakeholders. Those stakeholders included insurance companies; states committing to establish their own Insurance Marketplace; state Medicaid and CHIP programs trying to gauge the impact to their existing programs, policies, and systems; state departments of insurance; and many industry associations, some of which represented the agents and brokers that sold health insurance. That pace hampered abilities to drill to greater levels of details on requirements which also made it difficult to refine budgeting and contracting strategies.

The other reality was one where my staff, contractors, and several other like-minded people lived. We possessed a healthy respect for how difficult the next three years would be, and that respect had us always looking for opportunities to buy back time and to buy down risk. In other words, we needed to factor in the pace that alternate reality was moving and not choose technologies, solutions, and approaches to systems development that would take more time than needed.

Gross oversimplification took center stage about thirty days post-launch, when the "tech surge" arrived, shepherded by Todd Park, who at the time was the federal CTO. Mikey Dickerson, a Google employee that took a leave of absence to be a part of the surge, proclaimed to the masses that what they and the rest of the surge came to do was not really that hard because, after all, HealthCare.gov is "just a website." People in the tech community drank that up like free beer. This contributed to the frenzy about why the tech effort failed so miserably if we're only talking about a website. The distortion and oversimplification avoided explaining the circumstances that led up to the launch, which would have provided greater transparency and promoted deeper understanding of the issues so lessons could be learned and benefit future similar endeavors. Perhaps it didn't matter to most about what transpired prior to launch because people wanted a simpler and more easily digestible narrative than what the truth would have provided. While I totally get that perspective, I also believe there are so many valuable lessons to share including a more comprehensive explanation of how events transpired rather than just a point-in-time analysis.

What about the previous three years? What did it take to stand there in the middle of 2010 and deliver an MVP coexisting with an alternate reality, trudging through one of the most toxic political climates in memorable history?

In 2010, there may have been only a handful of people in the federal government who recognized, appreciated, and had a healthy respect for the undertaking of this effort. Coming up with a better way to solve a problem requires a serious and realistic appreciation for both the present state of where you're at in time and the available capabilities and what has to be in place as the MVP at some future date. We started on the program in mid-2010, and the imposed target date for the MVP was October 1, 2013.

MAKING TECHNOLOGY CHOICES THAT MATCH THE CIRCUMSTANCE

When looking for the most appropriate solutions for building the necessary systems, a lot of companies come knocking and try to convince you that their product is the "best." Of course, their pitches came with success stories from other sectors, clients, types of business, and government agencies. While past performance was important, like the stock market, it did not guarantee future performance, especially since the business context was different and unlike anything that existed in the market.

Applying the appropriate solution in a given context is rooted in how well you understand requirements and surrounding factors affecting the collective ability to obtain "implementable requirements" in an environment impacted by political agendas, institutionalized inefficiencies, technical debt, and lack of clarity and consistency in who actually has the final say in scoping the MVP. Regardless of technology choices, you minimally have to understand high-level requirements. Low-level requirements in this case were trapped in an alternate reality that was unstable or nonexistent in terms of sharing with the technical staff.

That meant working with what we had, stepping back and seeing that the high-level requirements could provide a relatively firm basis from which to make assumptions on network, hosting, compute, storage, operating systems, environments, etc. Those were some of the things in the technical domain that my team had greater control over, so we used our collective experience and the best available information about the program to make broad assumptions to build a reference architecture for a cloud-based implementation and take advantage of the flexibility of Infrastructure as a Service (IaaS) and elasticity to get an early start in hopes of maximizing what we already knew was going to be an extremely time constrained situation.

Cloud computing in 2010 had just made its presence known in the federal government, and one of the key guides from the first federal CIO, Vivek Kundra, was his "cloud-first policy" described in the document "25 Point Implementation Plan to Reform Federal Information Technology Management," published in December 2010. While the policy was somewhat revolutionary, it lacked specifics such as guidance for agencies with critical applications processing sensitive data to select and work with Cloud service providers to ensure FISMA compliance. FISMA, the Federal Information Security Management Act, defined the framework to protect government information, operations, and assets against threats. The cloud-first policy was issued pre-FedRAMP (Federal Risk and Authorization Management Program) days, and the General Services Administration (GSA) had only a shell of a vehicle in which it was only in the early stages to onboard certain "qualified" cloud providers, not that anyone knew what the terms "qualified," "certified," or "accredited" meant in the 2010–2012 timeframe. With a little help from Pete Tseronis, who at the time was a senior advisor at the Department of Energy providing us with an example of a Infrastructure-as-a-Service contract template, we had a precedent to us in setting up our initial contract engagement with a Cloud service provider.

Several of us on the team had extensive experience working with hosting providers and have toured and assessed dozens of data centers around the country. Working with Intel, Cisco, and NetApp in early 2011, we determined that Terremark in Culpeper, Virginia, was a facility that could handle the demands of the Insurance Marketplace program and readily implement the reference architecture. We had considered Amazon Web Services (AWS) and met with the team several times toward the end of 2010, but at that time, AWS only hosted low-risk FISMA government applications such as email. So we went with what was the best available and would meet the federal security requirements under FISMA for at least a "moderate" application—we didn't have the luxury of betting on AWS becoming the juggernaut it is now as a cloud service provider.

The reference architecture that my team developed was based on what were solid high-level requirements, or at least what we considered valid assumptions within our technical domain. The assumptions included known elements of the core functions the systems had to perform.

My experience working in both Medicaid and Medicare gave me an understanding of how health insurance, health plans, access to health insurance, affordability models based on subsidized premiums and cost sharing, eligibility verifications and determinations, enrollment functions, health plan management, payment functions, HIPAA electronic data interchange standard transactions and code sets, roles and functions of insurance regulators, and all aspects of health-care operations and the daily, weekly, monthly, and annual processing cycles determined by the business process execution requirements. The Insurance Marketplace program leveraged the individual and small group markets but recalibrated the rules to comply with essential health benefits, APTC, cost-sharing reductions, risk adjustment, reinsurance, and many other insurance reform requirements. It still was essentially a health plan product developed and offered by insurance companies leveraging much of their existing provider networks. To meet ACA requirements as a QHP, it had to follow a slightly modified and accelerated process for submission, review, and approval by the insurance commissioners in the states in which their products were to be sold. Add to that the ACA requirements for an online, real-time capability to apply, shop, and enroll in a health plan and you have the set of high-level requirements and assumptions from which to determine the design of the major components that will make up what is simplistically referred to as HealthCare.gov.

The IRS and other federal agencies played a significant role in the ACA Insurance Marketplace program on key requirements that are specifically called out within the law. For instance, the IRS calculates the APTC, and the information provided by the applicant online must be checked against the federal authoritative source of the data. In other words, a valid Social Security number (SSN) must be with the agency that "owns" the data, referred to within the federal government as systems of record (SOR) data. Other applicant information had to be verified in conjunction with the DHS and the SSA for lawful presence in the United States, Medicare coverage status, DoD for military health and Tricare coverage, VA coverage, OPM for federal employee and retiree coverage, and the Peace Corps for coverage of its staff. This was another pool of significant challenges on many fronts.

First, each federal agency assesses the sensitivity levels of the data the agency is collecting, processing, storing, and exchanging and makes risk-based decisions on how to best implement security requirements within the context of their programs, policies and requirements for ensuring privacy protections of the data they handle. What may seem to be similar in terms of risk can result in different implementations of security and privacy requirements between different agencies. Because of varying risk acceptances across government and non-government organizations, these differences must be factored in when developing agreements prior to conducting a data exchange to ensure that the organizations will comply with each other's security and privacy policies governing the data. The technical teams, security teams, and business teams work together to assess the risks that are involved and the business teams take the lead in any final determination of what risk acceptances, mitigations, and corrective actions that need to be taken to appropriately apply the best level of security and privacy protections for the technical and administrative aspects of the security and privacy program.

Imagine the thousands of federal programs that are supported by tens of thousands of systems that do not all have data with equal characteristics and sensitivity levels. Aside from figuring out the governance framework for all of these dissimilar security and privacy rules, the major issue with interfacing with so many agencies was that each agency and each program that operates systems are driven by their own dependencies, business processes, and schedules. The expected user experience on HealthCare.gov was interaction in real time; as they filled out an online application, all the data inputted in the browser was being verified by each agency. In 2010, the vast majority of the uses of these federal agencies' authoritative data sources were not online, real-time experiences. In fact, interacting with an agency and data source usually meant receiving a batch file on a weekly or monthly basis.

To overcome the unevenness of the policies across the agencies and to support an online, real-time user experience, my team and I determined the most efficient and optimal way accessing the required federal authoritative data that resided behind the firewalls of all the involved federal agencies by the Insurance Marketplaces in real time demanded the design and implementation of a federal data services hub. From concept to reality, the Federal Data Services Hub, or Hub for short, provided all the involved federal agencies a single point for coordinating service levels, operational schedules, and brokering interconnection agreements, and data use agreements so each agency did not have to directly manage a significant increase in their individual point-to-point connections. And for the states that are part of the FFM, or operating their own SBMs, and state agencies administering the Medicaid and CHIP programs also benefitted from the increased efficiencies of not having to individually negotiate with each of the involved federal agencies. The Hub also had file transfer capabilities and an EDI interface engine so that batch exchanges were facilitated as well as the requirements to convert XML to HIPAA EDI standard for health plan enrollment transactions to be sent to insurance companies to kick off their processes to onboard the member/consumer.

The hub concept was not a new one; it had been implemented before but never at such scale in the federal government and not in a manner that supported an online consumer enrollment process and the data exchanges necessary to move their information to an insurance company. It was a new way to do things, and it worked nearly flawlessly.

The Hub used the same reference architecture and cloud environment as the FFM. While the requirements, relatively speaking, were less complex than for the FFM, it was a critical part of HealthCare.gov and serves the program well to this day.

After the rollout of HealthCare.gov, I found it extremely interesting that so many "experts" jumped in and provided their opinions on what went wrong. It made me wonder what their point of reference was in coming up with solutions that sounded so simple, as if building a new house where no houses exist is the same as building a house where entire neighborhoods with utilities, roads, and infrastructure already exist, when actually the checklist for building a house in, say, Maryland is not the same as building a house in a remote area of Alaska. While conceptually you are still building a house, in reality it involves other major factors.

ALL THE PERPETRATORS OF WHAT IS DEFENDED AS IDEOLOGICALLY CORRECT FOR A POLITICAL PARTY BUT MORALLY WRONG FOR YOUR FELLOW MAN WANT YOU TO BELIEVE THAT THE PROBLEM AND THE SOLUTION IS SIMPLE.

Oversimplification of the HealthCare.gov rollout was an insult to people's intelligence and to the thousands of people across the United States who worked on some aspect of it. It also perpetuated the myth that technology is always the culprit whenever there is a problem, so that's where to look when a project goes south.

No, it can't be the bad politics or the holy war over whether health care is a right or a privilege. All the perpetrators of what is defended as ideologically correct for a political party but morally wrong for your fellow man want you to believe that the problem and the solution is simple. It's the "build the wall and our problems are over" approach to explaining complex problems. Perhaps this was just one of many glimpses of the circumstances we have come to live in today.

THE HAZARDS ASSOCIATED WITH STANDARDIZATION

When I became the CTO of CMS in 2008, one of my primary objectives was to continue the work of my predecessor in expanding the standards that are an integral part of how an organization governs its IT practices and processes at the enterprise level. CMS already published a first version of a technical reference architecture (TRA), but the pace of change and ever-increasing diversity—driven by expanding portfolios of work in all parts of Medicare, Medicaid, tech refreshes of end-of-life hardware and software, and shifting from physical servers to virtual servers for certain types of workloads—demanded a major revision of the TRA. The situation also demanded a greater level of detail to guide implementers such as systems architects, engineers, developers, security professionals, software vendors, and data center operators.

Looking at the agency's enterprise needs and assessing how to create more standardization, stability, and predictability in how the IT organization supported various programs and projects was absolutely the right thing to do. Best practices guidance from industry experts, analysts, auditors, and the Software Engineering Institute all pointed to the need to adopt a rigorous discipline throughout the life cycle of a project, from inception to disposition. In any effort to create uniformity, consistency, and predictability, there may also be downsides as the repeatable practice and processes governing the life cycle becomes blind to key differentiators that speak to the need for a revised or renewed sense that new business challenges may require the process to recognize and adapt to the changing complexion of the problem.

We build organizations and staff them with competent professionals and also outsource work to companies that provide the experience not available in-house. These professionals and companies hone their skills and competencies for years on specific disciplines, products, and services. The architects, application developers, business analysts, requirements managers, project managers, testers, quality analysts, and others fine-tune their specific disciplines within a process that wants to standardize as much as possible. The practice in itself is not a bad thing. The problem is that, as people and organizations become tuned for similar patterns of requirements or "work," there is a tendency to treat every problem as if it has already been solved before. Sticking with what is familiar may not be the lowest-risk approach in designing a solution.

For example, very large systems integrators or IT contractors maintain their competitive edge in part due to how they have optimized their proposal and solution development practices. The approach and choices of tools such as application development frameworks, database platforms, commercial off-the-shelf products, testing tools, hosting arrangements, etc. are closely examined and tuned with an emphasis on managing cost. While this approach isn't necessarily standardization, it does share similarities with organizations that strive to achieve uniformity and consistency, which in this example is "standardization" for the sake of managing cost.

Another example of standardization is the government procurement process. When the government puts forth a solicitation for bidders to provide support and services, particularly in software development, the government's perspective is shrouded in something called "best value," which is a way to say that: amongst all the bidders, the government will select the best technical proposal, relative to cost. This can translate into a situation where the most technically superior response with the highest cost may not be of "best value" when compared to a technically adequate, but lower cost response. The procurement process also strives to achieve uniformity and consistency, which is not necessarily a bad thing except when the process become more important to maintain than what comes out of the process.

Establishing and applying standards to improve an organization's life cycle governance process, a contractor's Request for Proposal (RFP) process, or a government agency's procurement process to promote repeatable practices and processes, is not in itself a bad thing. I just want to share my observation that often in establishing, adhering, and enforcing a process, an organization can quickly lose sight of what actually is coming out of the process and perhaps, even more detrimental, is becoming entrenched in the process and failing to recognize and adapt to change.

In 2005, I was working on Medicare Part D, which required over a dozen systems to adapt to new requirements stemming from a new prescription drug program. There was a need to reimagine the scale, volume, and performance of all of the hardware, software, network, batch processing, and real-time processing—basically every aspect of how CMS conducted its IT investments, operations, and expectations that aligned with how the programs were changing. Around that time, I noticed a pattern in the practice of designing individual applications with highly dedicated relational data models that were built using relational database management systems (RDBMS) to further optimize processing and storage. The approach worked well for each individual system, but at an enterprise level, when trying to integrate different datasets from multiple systems, over time it became quite inefficient as more and more integrations were created and maintained. Using relational database technology is also highly beneficial if there is a good grasp on the data and datatypes that the system will need to handle, but in most projects that I've participated in, policy making and getting regulations finalized impact the stability of requirements. And that impacts the ability to build a stable and efficient data model.

When I recognized the problem, I began a habit of avoiding going straight to the conclusion that every system in the world that was built or would be built must use RDBMS technology. That's when I realized that, particularly for an enterprise as large as CMS, spending over $3 billion annually on maintaining and building systems driven by ever-changing policies and regulations, there needed to be a certain amount of controlled diversity in the technologies used to meet the challenges of new health-care programs.

When I became the CIO for OCIIO in July 2010, I started to witness firsthand just how insane the struggle would be in the coming years, and not just with unclear budget, contracting, and hiring strategies. By January 2011, when we were moved to CMS, for me, it was like going home after five mo-nths. However, I could already see that the insanity and lack of clarity around the specific policies and priorities of the program would be the root cause of our collective inability to get from policy creation and regulation to detailed guidance and requirements to development and implementation in an expedient manner.

The only thing left to do was embrace the reality. There was no running away or hiding from this destiny.

One of the key criticisms of the technologies used behind the FFM or HealthCare.gov regarded the decision to use database technology based on NoSQL technology, which in this case was the selection of MarkLogic as the database platform for the FFM. In early 2011, I had experienced almost an entire year of chaotic uncertainty on budgets, contracts, policies, and sharing minimal information with stakeholders, and by then, recognized that the situation would remain unchanged for the foreseeable future. But there was a moment of clear recognition that we had to truly adapt to the circumstances at hand with how risky the project had already become with shifting or unclear priorities and lack of progress in nailing down requirements. Based on what I'd experienced, the best course of action and lowest risk approach was to not proceed as usual, defaulting to using RDBMS technology simply because we were familiar and had enterprise licenses. I committed to using NoSQL technology along with other technology choices and design decisions based on the realities of the situation at hand.

IT'S ALWAYS A BALANCING ACT

The key is to stabilize and have a core set of competencies built around technology standards. Then, when a new set of challenges comes along, recognize the magnitude of change demanded. How well you see that is a function of how open you are to recognizing whether the new challenge is best managed with existing technologies that your organization has already invested in, new technologies it is considering adopting, or a blend of old and new technologies that can withstand the uncertainty of meeting the requirements and adapting to volatile situations. For example, choosing a NoSQL database when you know early on that the final requirements for specific data collected during the online enrollment process come very late—with HealthCare.gov, the dataset was not fully approved by OMB until around February 2013, months before the launch date.

Given that there were requirements to retain source application information to transfer it to respective states for individuals to determine Medicaid or CHIP eligibility, the document aspect of NoSQL databases also provided a greater chance that relevant and related data would not be lost when building custom extract, transform, and load (ETL) jobs reassembling data residing in an RDBMS. But there was unbelievable pushback from developers and database administrators who did not comprehend the volatility of the requirements and the unimaginable frenzy that two builds each day would produce in the last ninety days preceding the launch.

Even in late 2011, when few specifics were known about the types of data that would be used in the program, a fair number of people immediately dismissed the notion of NoSQL. They wanted to conclude that a relational database must be used because it worked and there was a large supply of technical professionals with relational database experience.

What puzzled me was that we had discussed that a best practice from lessons learned was to always ask up front "What problem are we trying to solve?" before leaping to conclusions about what technologies to use. Moreover, having directly witnessed, reviewed, critiqued, and provided recommendations as the CTO and chair of the technical review board (TRB) at CMS for several dozen major program and systems implementations, I knew that choosing technologies from a place of comfort was not a proven, risk-free approach.

Fully understanding the problem to be solved and the circumstances involved before selecting technologies is a much more reliable approach in reducing implementation risk. Taking that approach, learning that new challenges don't necessarily fit with a current approach is very difficult for a lot of organizations to do. It's like the old saying: "If all you have is a hammer, everything looks like a nail." Given the experience with the Insurance Marketplace program, particularly in the first two years and subsequently hearing lots of theories of what should have been done, I came up with my own version of that saying, actually related to a concept put forth by philosopher Abraham Kaplan and then disseminated in Abraham Maslow's book *The Psychology of Science* that refers to "an overdependence on a tried and true strategy or instrument, when another approach may be more suitable."[1] While you were busy polishing your golden hammer to take on a world full of nails, the world created the screw.

Using a standard "toolbox" of knowledge to tackle every problem can create a biased way of thinking. We've all also heard the phrase "Let's not try to boil the ocean." While that is a useful way to help people understand the scope of a problem, too often the phrase is used to constrain the range of possibilities so as not to waste precious time and resources trying to solve every problem that's related to the core issues at hand. But what if you aren't able to fathom the size or differentiate the vastness of the ocean with any other large body of water?

Whatever the challenge, it's about finding the best solution given the environment in which that challenge exists. With the ACA, that included all the uncertainty driven by politics, which then created a lot of indecision, volatility, and instability in getting policies and requirements in place so that there was actually something to build toward.

Trying to use old technologies for such a major new challenge would have been a huge mistake. That also meant that the systems

---

1   "Golden Hammer," Investopedia, accessed April 4, 2018, https://www.investopedia.com/terms/g/golden-hammer.asp.

development life cycle approach also had to be adapted to fit the circumstance.

ADOPTING THE LATEST TRENDS FOR THE GIVEN SITUATION

During the build of the Insurance Marketplace program, numerous people inquired about the use of agile. We adapted agile to the circumstances we were in. In fact, a few leads took the initiative to get certified as scrum masters and then introduced agile to the staff who were writing policy and regulations. The goal was to get an early start on documenting requirements that were known at the time, while working to adopt an agile approach to how they organized themselves around the dozens of regulations that had to be written with consideration for every other related regulation. Some of those could only move at the pace the policy and rule-making process moved, which was the quintessential example of a lumbering waterfall life cycle model. Add the toxic political environment to that slow grind and the result was a fragmented, no-detail approach to publishing regulations. Needless to say, that was highly detrimental to every stakeholder that was holding their breath waiting for more detail and clarity in order to plan and execute their respective pieces of the program.

Under normal conditions, the regulation process is followed by the next level of detail through what is called "sub-regulatory guidance." That can come in various forms—official letters from agency to agency or from agency to industry, marketing materials, conference presentations, briefings to various targeted audiences, and more. With the Insurance Marketplace program, there was an embedded fear among various leaders in the administration that sharing too much detail would provide ammunition for the Republicans to then recast in a bad light on a giant poster board on the House floor just how overly complicated Obamacare was.

That was part of the typical repertoire that Congressional representatives and their staffers used as part of the theatrics to drive a point about just how complex and fearful something was. Putting fear into the average American was a simple matter of blowing up a complicated diagram of the health-care system, thrusting it up for the people to see, and dropping the mic—political mission accomplished.

The fear of that happening was proven in the past in 1994 after President Bill Clinton announced his plan for health-care reform during the State of the Union Address. Senator Bob Dole, delivering the Republican response, displayed a giant poster board to illustrate the complicated boxes and lines that connected and intersected new, never before heard of organizations and functions that the Senator himself found difficult to understand. The idea was to show how the Clintons were going to make what was in such bad shape even worse. Indeed, that was a scare tactic. After that, the plans for health-care reform kept losing life. So in fear of material leaking and providing fodder for the republicans to display and scare people with, the sharing of technical diagrams, process and data flows,

> PUTTING FEAR INTO THE AVERAGE AMERICAN WAS A SIMPLE MATTER OF BLOWING UP A COMPLICATED DIAGRAM OF THE HEALTH CARE SYSTEM, THRUSTING IT UP FOR THE PEOPLE TO SEE, AND DROPPING THE MIKE—POLITICAL MISSION ACCOMPLISHED.

and PowerPoint presentations that contained such material were forbidden to be shared openly with other ACA stakeholders.

Between June and November of 2010, we at HHS worked closely with the IRS in an attempt to get an early start to document and create the high-level interactions, business processes, and overall EA, including the high-level decomposition of the major business areas that were needed to support the Insurance Marketplaces. All this work was ready to be shared with states through a collaboration platform that would help stakeholders align their efforts with ours, give them a head start in documenting their early assumptions, and minimize risk as much as possible. This was a very logical and necessary gesture to share what we had already developed, especially since we were providing states grant money to get their own early start in similar. Withholding the materials and not sharing with states created two effects. One was resentment because the states that were interested in establishing their own Insurance Marketplace knew we had been working on documenting the business processes and could not understand the logic behind us withholding, especially since these were not red states. The other effect was states then had to take some of the federal grant money and individually hired contractors to essentially recreate much of the same documentation for themselves. This lack of sharing really became burdensome when we would present and talk about the details at conferences but not distribute or make available any digital or paper copies of the very information we walked audiences through.

Ah, but leave it to creative and resourceful people to get things done. My staff and several policy teams conducted briefing sessions at conferences would use a "sticky wall" —an eight-foot-tall, twenty-foot-wide tacky surface on which they hung preprinted arrows, lines, and boxes and then walked through scenarios and process flows from beginning to end for a given business function. Afterwards, audience members took pictures with their phones and tablets—that's how we got documentation into their hands.

That is a small example of what it was like on a day-to-day basis working on the Insurance Marketplaces. If it had been a burger-cooking contest, it would be like the observers opining about why the result was such a sad-looking burger without looking in the kitchen and seeing that all the cooks had their hands and legs tied.

So, working under these constraints along with volatility and instability in how solid the requirements were in terms of being good enough to use in developing software are factors to consider when choosing technologies. But it's not the volatility or instability of the technology; it's the volatility and instability of obtaining information, detailing requirements, and then translating requirements into actual builds of software. People who debate the merits of one preferred technology over another often treat the situations as static and in a vacuum with no adverse environmental factors other than the pure technology play of what it can do or can't do. No technology can be insulated from poor or unclear requirements or the volatility created by a very hostile political environment.

By January 2013, the Republicans already had attempted to repeal Obamacare thirty-four times (the count would rise to fifty-four by 2014), and that fervor, or rather obsession, with overturning a basic aspect of living in a civilized society—to have health-care coverage—was done not for the good of the people, but only for their narrow constituencies and control, not unlike toddlers who haven't yet learned to cooperate and share. But many states with red governors added to the hostility by forbidding or even making it illegal for any state staff to work on ACA. While that might seem like an indicator of how many states HealthCare.gov would have to support, in fact many of the same governors who were publicly condemning Obamacare were also providing their signatures on grant proposals to HHS to receive millions of dollars to plan and maybe build their own SBM. States didn't formally declare whether they were opting to build their own SBM or letting HealthCare.gov be the storefront for their state until spring 2013.

Adding to the complexity of the state dimension of the project was the Supreme Court decision in summer 2012 allowing states to opt out of Medicaid expansion. Medicaid expansion was the part of ACA in addition to the Insurance Marketplaces that would be the avenue for getting more of the uninsured covered under more generous and nationally consistent income-based eligibility rules. The Supreme Court decision created another layer of complexity, because for states that opted out of expansion but still wanted HealthCare.gov to be their storefront, we had to handle the inconsistent set of income-based eligibility rules of the non-expansion states with the consistent rules of the expansion states.

For example, the Insurance Marketplace online application accommodates all members of a household who wish to be covered by health insurance. But the composition of the household can be made up of potentially Medicaid eligible, CHIP, or APTC-qualified people and people that may have coverage through other federal programs such as Medicare, Tricare, VA, Office of Personnel Management (OPM), and the Peace Corps. While not all applications will represent the entire range of possible types of eligibility, the majority of applications handled by HealthCare.gov are not simple ones. It had to apply rules to the entire application and applicant, and also break out the individuals within an application/household to determine how each should be handled in enrolling for health-care coverage. The income threshold rules for Medicaid in an expansion state and Medicaid in a non-expansion state had to be coordinated, then individuals on an application processed and handed off to the state for additional processing and disposition versus others on the application who may continue to a Marketplace enrollment with APTCs.

Outside of the people and organizations that work on these programs, very few people are aware of this level of complexity. They don't understand that the laws and regulations that govern these programs are in place largely so that people can get coverage through at least one means, to reduce the number of multiple enrollments that don't enhance coverage, and to protect the government from paying out subsidies to people who are already receiving health-care coverage via another federal program.

A CULTURAL ISSUE

Too often when old understanding keeps being applied to new challenges, it's at least in part due to organizational cultural issues.

Everyone wants to feel like they're contributing to something when they go to work. We build our careers around the expertise and experience gained through training, observation, participation, and trial by fire, and it is quite natural to have a sense of pride in what we achieve. Organizations that have multiple IT support departments dedicated to specific business units and program areas often wind up building and supporting similar IT capabilities. Whether it's application development, data and database management, digital services, infrastructure, or data centers, there is inevitably some level of unnecessary redundancy that creates confusion and lack of transparency as to the reasons that justify both initial and ongoing funding to further perpetuate the sprawl. It's particularly confusing for external customers, because these duplicative efforts create different entry points for the same customer segment to engage and do business. Yet when it's suggested that a problem be looked at from a different perspective, people are not immediately open to the idea. Typically, they start off feeling threatened—maybe even a little derided—that after all the rewards and accolades, all the raises and promotions, now suddenly what they know isn't good enough to solve the problem at hand. It's an emotional reaction.

A lot of working on large, complex programs with so many people involved is about first getting everyone to lower their armor, so to speak. Innate bias toward the familiar creates a shield around us, keeping us comfortably grounded in what we know we know. When a significant change comes about or is discussed as a group, too often a polarization effect happens, where people who clearly have done well repeating their pattern of "I've seen problems like this before, so therefore I know what the answer is" can feel like they're under a spotlight, because the discussion of novel ideas and approaches collides with their grounded sense of self built on real-world experiences. That triggers a personal sense of challenge; defense mechanisms kick in, and the reaction can range from stoic silence to outright shouting to overpower a conversation.

It is important to have ownership in what you do, but at the end of the day, it's not about the individual, especially in government, where you don't own anything—not the desk you're sitting at, the office you're sitting in, the space you occupy each day. All you own is the privilege of working on behalf of the public. People in government tend to forget that. When multiple people begin to band together in their firm belief of the better way to solve a problem, things can become a tribal turf battle, like a bad game of *Survivor*. When tribes compete to win their respective way of solving a problem, it becomes all about winning for the teams and not what it should be, which is doing what is best for the situation and the public being served.

BE OPEN TO POSSIBILITIES

The key is to avoid plateauing in your base of knowledge. I have always believed that there is no "full" line to learning and acquiring knowledge. The difficulty is in believing in the possibility of continuous learning and opening yourself up to acquire new information and knowledge. In the IT professions, it's important to constantly refresh skills and knowledge to solve contemporary problems, to learn not just from your experiences, but also from other people outside your area (other areas of government, the commercial world, etc.). Then, building off that knowledge base can enable you to make decisions about dealing with highly complex programs. Truly great IT professionals are not just acquiring new knowledge within their own technical domain, but more so are acquiring knowledge of the business domain they are supporting. Seeing and understanding the possibilities of the complementary relationships between business and technical domains is integral to a successful technology career. If you practice it with due diligence, it becomes a cornerstone in building trust and confidence across your teams and with your customers. It's not about taking more courses or going to more conferences or training. To improve your overall knowledge and ability to be a critical thinker, and to solve problems in an adaptive way that accounts for changes that you've never seen before, you must open your mind. It doesn't mean learning more of the same things.

Your ability to solve problems effectively won't just come from knowledge from both the technical and business domains. A critical ingredient is creativity and the use of your imagination to think about what is possible in a given situation. I find that in many ways, the energy and enthusiasm for solving problems does not come from always operating in a crisis-induced, adrenaline junkie mode, although on occasion I have considered that it was possible I was attracted to messy situations. The triggers that automatically turn on your energy and enthusiasm may very well come from that creative part of you that can imagine the possible ways to solve a problem. Whenever I feel that creativity stirring in my brain, my energy levels automatically elevate. When colleagues and friends sync up to that energy, then really great things start to happen. The numbness and lack of enthusiastic response that comes from solving problems in a robotic manner, repeating the patterns over and over again, will disappear.

Tapping into your creative side may require a break in the routine and using other parts of your brain to help elevate your thinking prowess. For example, I participated in several art classes learning how to create mosaics, stained glass, sculpture, engraving, silk screening T-shirt designs, and my favorite, bronze casting. I believe these classes helped me significantly in stimulating other parts of my brain and allowing me to expand my imagination for what was possible. While there is no scientific study conducted with empirical data to back up my thesis, I've found that learning and acquiring knowledge can be a rote exercise that reinvigorates my creative side to really help balance out the chaos.

One of the biggest lessons I learned while working on the Medicare Prescription Drug Program was to have a strong appreciation for what each participant or stakeholder is experiencing in the larger picture to understand how all the pieces do or don't work for the person center stage. When I was called upon to fully immerse myself in the final year of Part D and what was left to be developed and implemented, I worked with a team of dedicated people at CMS. They developed solutions and processes to help Medicare save money by avoiding payments for health-care services that should have been paid for by another insurer, such as an employer-sponsored health plan. It was an extensive, national-level operation involving billions of eligibility and claims records to be processed in batch mode while applying complex business rules to find situations where Medicare should not have paid first or paid at all.

We were collectively trying to apply that cost-avoidance or coordination-of-benefits (COB) approach to solving a similar problem in the Part D program. The complex rules for coverage of the prescription drug benefit changed depending on where a beneficiary was in their drug spend. This had to be accurately tracked so that they could receive the correct coverage levels as they increased their drug spend and encountered a coverage gap—called the "donut hole" in Part D. The Part D plan that had the enrollment was required to keep track of that spend data on a real-time basis, which is how the prescription drug claims are adjudicated. It took some time to convince people that working on COB issues in a health-care services world meant that much of the data processing is able to tolerate lags in information and data because the business process was designed not to have a final answer the day the health-care service occurred. To do so, the system would have

> TO IMPROVE YOUR OVERALL KNOWLEDGE AND ABILITY TO BE A CRITICAL THINKER, AND TO SOLVE PROBLEMS IN AN ADAPTIVE WAY THAT ACCOUNTS FOR CHANGES THAT YOU'VE NEVER SEEN BEFORE, YOU MUST OPEN YOUR MIND. IT DOESN'T MEAN LEARNING MORE OF THE SAME THINGS.

to coordinate: the processing of eligibility, coverage, and reimbursement information from primary and secondary insurance policies; contracted rates with providers that were in or out of network; and utilization limits such as number of hospital days or number of MRIs in a given period of time, to name a few.

Compare that to how patients usually get their prescription drugs filled in a retail setting and you start to understand that one type of health-care billing works in non-real time and the other works in real time. That happens because the pharmacy is nested in a retail establishment, where the typical customer is accustomed to walking up to a point-of-sale (POS) system, paying for their products, and leaving the store in a relatively short time and without having to receive a letter saying they owe more than what they paid in the store. Recognizing this difference between how health-care services are delivered and prescription drugs are dispensed and paid for was crucial for determining what the suitable solutions would be.

I used to conduct a new employee orientation session where I asked the audience whether they ever thought about the difference between getting prescriptions filled and paying a final, calculated copay or coinsurance amount before you leave the pharmacy, and visiting a doctor or hospital, paying a co-pay or coinsurance, and then days or weeks later receiving an invoice of balances due for services that were either not fully covered or because you received a procedure earlier in the plan year where you may not have met a deductible. I found it very interesting how one's own experiences with the health-care system, good and bad, can sometimes be a little disconnected from efforts at work to develop policies, processes, and procedures that ultimately impact people's experience with the health-care system in the real world. We all eventually recognize the irony of having to someday live and abide by the policies and procedures we had a hand in creating.

In working with various policy teams and stakeholders on the ACA Insurance Marketplace program, we all tried to be mindful of the perspectives of people who were uninsured or had sporadic health-care coverage throughout their lives. When you have not had consistent coverage, your frame of reference and ability to navigate the process to apply, enroll, select, and utilize health care can be quite different than people who had been insured their entire lives, which interestingly enough, does not automatically mean they understand how to best navigate and utilize their health care.

BE WILLING TO LEARN

A report issued by the Office of the Inspector General (OIG) that looked back at the HealthCare.gov rollout noted that people didn't have skills around the technologies selected for the program. That's true, but it's not the whole story. It wasn't that people just didn't have the skills, it's that they were also unwilling to learn. Adopting new database technologies was risky, but the full story is about the inability to see what solutions a new problem actually requires.

If not enough people understand a technology, it might be that it's not a popular choice, or in some instances it's a matter of people claiming that the technology won't work and then avoiding the use of it for the sake of the old ways. The reality is that if they made a decent attempt to examine the possibilities, they might discover that it actually does solve some new problems.

Similarly, the whole story wasn't shared in an article in *Time* magazine that looked at how a team came in and "rescued" Health-Care.gov. For starters, it's easy for a team to come in after the fact on any project and say, "We wouldn't have done it that way." But that's not taking into account the experience of having been there for the three years that the program was being built or of being there for more than a decade in advance and watching other problems unfold and recognizing that this new problem was going to be messy. It didn't take into account that decisions made along the way were all about adapting to the volatility in order to have a basis upon which to correct and create stability.

I was invited to speak to a small group of leaders from various ministries of the government of Singapore on the story behind the rollout of HealthCare.gov. Afterwards, one of the executives asked about the rescue effort. Before I gave her my answer, I asked her if she had ever encountered a situation where after all the tough work of getting to day one, others then joined and helped with stabilizing the effort. Yes, she replied, that had happened several times.

Then I asked her if she had read the story in *Time* (she had) and if there was, in all of her experiences in launching a program, a technology and implementation situation so dire that could realistically be salvaged around in sixty-three days—especially one the size and scope of HealthCare.gov. She thought about it for a few seconds and then realized how unbelievable the narrative really was. I shared with her that if people such as herself, with similar firsthand experience, thought about the story for a minute, they would realize that it was incomplete—it did not tell the whole story. She then agreed that the narrative was a major injustice to all the people who had devoted their lives for four years to make HealthCare.gov happen. Instead of telling the real story of their efforts, it portrayed that a small team made a miraculous rescue of something as simple as a "website." She agreed that, to her team, that would have been demeaning and demoralizing.

She couldn't have described it better.

CHAPTER 4

CONTEXT AND SCALE MATTER

When several of us started the IT organization in OCIIO, there were more ACA initiatives than just the Insurance Marketplaces. While the office that was responsible for the Insurance Marketplace program was in the spotlight most often, OCIIO had the Office of Oversight responsible for key insurance reforms such as medical loss ratio and rate review and the Office of Insurance Programs, which supported the Pre-existing Condition Insurance Plan (PCIP) to ensure that every state had a high-risk pool plan so that people such as chronically ill children could have coverage even though they had high health-care costs.

OCIIO also started with an Office of Consumer Support, which initiated a consumer assistance program around the summer of 2010. One of the initiatives under that program was to work with every state to establish an ombudsman at the state insurance commissioner's office to serve as an advocate for consumer issues with insurance companies. As the IT organization for OCIIO, we were expected to cover all the IT needs of all the ACA initiatives the office was charged with.

My team met with two business leads from the consumer assistance area to determine their needs for bringing up the ombudsman program in each state. They both indicated that a website was needed to serve as the means for each state's ombudsman to submit complaint and tracking information to CCIIO as well as to support collaboration across the states. One of the leads indicated that she was a web designer and actually had a web design business before she came to work at OCIIO. That was encouraging, since not only would the leads provide the requirements and content, they also had an expert who could work on design and user experience. When the discussion came to budget, they indicated they were planning on $10,000. I knew as soon as I heard that figure that we were going to have some difficulty in agreeing on what is involved when the federal government puts up a website that is expected to register and authenticate users and manage their access; collect, process and store sensitive data; withstand the rigors of security policies under FISMA; and adhere to the clearance process and public notice process for federal systems that collect information.

The model they were familiar with in the commercial world was to go to a service provider, register a domain name, and receive a URL. They might also have the provider host a website using its templates and adding content to create the site. No security testing, no public notices, no great level of authentication, etc.

From there, the discussion just went downhill. Our respective experiences working with website projects were similar in general terms of what purposes a website can serve and the high level of functionality a website can offer. But that's where the similarities ended, because there are differentiators when it comes to volume, complexity, security, compliance with Section 508 of the Rehabilitation Act, and other factors that drive design and implementation approaches between private sector and public sector.

The considerations for context and scale are key in understanding why government does things a little differently and helps explain why certain comparisons between private and public sector IT projects are not an apples-to-apples situation.

It can be challenging to compare federal government websites to those in the commercial world. First of all, they abide by two different sets of security and privacy rules. When Facebook wants to update its privacy policy, all it has to do is provide you with a disclosure of the policy and ask for your acknowledgment. Practically no one reads the disclosure; most people just click right on through, and then their shopping and viewing habits are tracked and shared. A range of laws regarding the collection, storage, and disclosure of people's information restricts the federal government from doing the same for commercial purposes. The privacy and security laws, regulations, and specific agreements to share data completely alter the considerations for collecting only the necessary data to conduct business with the government.

Case in point: Toward the end of HHS secretary Mike Leavitt's service (2005–2009), there was a concerted push toward promoting the Medicare beneficiary population's access to a personal health record (PHR). PHRs in 2009 were mostly commercially supported by health plans as an added service to their members, but almost two-thirds of Medicare beneficiaries were not in a health plan benefit. This represented an opportunity for many interested companies, one of which was Google. As CTO, I was tasked to work with CMS's Office of E-Health Standards to conduct a series of working sessions to see how Google would be able to securely provide a PHR service to Medicare beneficiaries.

The first few meetings, I went over some of the minimum requirements the federal government imposes on any other organization that is authorized to receive and store personally identifiable information (PII) and personal health information (PHI) data from Medicare. Typically, the minimum requirements involve data use agreements (DUAs), data breach notification procedures, agreement to be subjected to audits, and providing documentation of internal controls and procedures for handling data. It became apparent after the second or third call that Google was not ready to meet these minimum requirements. A couple of years later, Google decided to step away from the PHR business. That is not to say that Google wasn't savvy enough or made some kind of error in judgment. Google is in business to grow revenue and value in the company and can't really stay in business or be profitable if it invests in ventures that have little to no potential for revenue.

When the government develops and implements policies and technologies to start a program for the public, the motivation is quite different, even though both private and public endeavors strive to be successful but defined in their own context. That is the central difference between commercial businesses and the government. What motivates an organization to be successful in its own right depends on how it defines success. If protecting people's privacy is paramount, a business would be motivated in similar manner as the government.

Take, for example, all the popular social media sites that have redefined our experiences and expectations using the Internet and how an entire generation doesn't even think twice about sharing their daily experiences with the world. In that context, where these businesses have experienced huge success, would every aspect of how they became successful automatically then become the model for government? It may not be reasonable or logical to think that 100 percent of what made a business successful can be replicated within the government. Catchy phrases heard at political rallies such as "Run the government like a business" sound like a novel approach to governing but in reality, would place the interests driven by profit motives over and above what would be in the public's interest.

Not all comparisons between the private- and public-sector technology efforts are invalid. Having served in CTO, deputy CIO, and CIO positions in the federal government, I always believed that no one organization or product vendor had all the answers. That meant building relationships with other government agencies, industry, research services, standards development organizations, and trade associations to hear about potentially similar situations and what was done or learned to solve problems.

Part of the learning was to understand and gain an appreciation of not just how a given problem was solved but also the context, scale, and level of complexity that was involved. That then properly frames whether there's much to learn and borrow. It is very time consuming to build a wide range of relationships and to try to learn enough about what others do in similar or different situations, but you also have a much better chance of getting closer to an apples-to-apples comparison in this approach.

ONE BITE AT A TIME

Getting everyone on board with the micro details of a project requires having someone shepherd the build-out of the system and being able to trace it all the way back to the requirements.

Once you understand and appreciate the context, particularly the business and political contexts you factor into your approach in developing solutions, you have a more realistic sense of how far you have to travel between your starting point and where you need to be at a particular date in the future.

The best example of the need to understand the context, the starting point, and the ending point from a business perspective, is the guaranteed issuance provision of the ACA. That was a key business process change in the health insurance industry—no one could be denied coverage for a preexisting condition. Prior to October 1, 2013, the capability to shop for health-care coverage online existed, but with one major difference having to do with medical underwriting. In a non-guaranteed issuance situation, meaning you could be denied for preexisting conditions, when you shopped online at a number of online insurance brokerages or insurance companies and found premiums quoted, they were still subject to medical underwriting. That could mean requests for your health record, a physical exam, blood work, and potentially other tests to assess the risk in selling health insurance coverage to you.

Prior to ACA, that underwriting process could take thirty days or longer, depending on your health conditions and lifestyle. So, yes, you could shop online, but you were not able to complete the enrollment into health-care coverage until the underwriting process was complete and rendered either an actual premium that correlated with the risk in covering you, or a denial of coverage due to "preexisting conditions." The entire delivery chain—from product development to processing your application for coverage to actually quoting a premium and then agreeing to enroll you so that you could access the benefits—moved at the speed of the underwriting process. You could shop online, have a great experience, peruse lots of insurance products that matched your needs, apply for coverage, and then wait thirty days or more to find out whether you would be accepted for coverage. If accepted, then you would get the actual premium amount.

Just consider the business process change that was involved in how the ACA required guaranteed issuance. That meant that every process that needed to drive an accurate quote of risk and premium would have to be done up front and serve a real-time experience where a consumer could shop and complete the enrollment process and right away know the specific premiums they would be paying. This was highly disruptive considering the existing model of purchasing health insurance.

Understanding this one requirement and its implications out of thousands of requirements allowed for a true appreciation of the path that needed to be taken from how it worked at the starting point to how it needed to work at a point in the future. Fully understanding this one major requirement under ACA then informed us of the interdependencies with other requirements, so that we could factor that into the technical design that was people/consumer-facing and non-consumer-facing (the "back end") and know what the trade-offs were to effectively focus on the MVP.

It's crucial to see the big picture as well as the parts that make up the big picture. That means understanding the relative size and scope of a project and then decomposing it into workable pieces. When it comes to super-scale program initiatives such as ACA, all it takes is looking at the big picture to realize that every capability can't be delivered at the same time. It's not even about having enough resources or time. It's about being able to identify the business details—the requirements that come out of the policymaking process—before being able to effectively and efficiently design systems, develop software, and understand the trade-offs that will inevitably occur.

Without both the large and small pieces, it becomes nearly impossible to understand and appreciate exactly what's at hand in any given situation. Sometimes it isn't an elephant you are trying to "eat," but rather a herd of elephants. That's what it was like implementing the ACA.

HEALTH CARE ONLINE—2010 VERSION VERSUS 2013 VERSION

The ACA required the secretary of HHS to establish a "portal" where consumers could peruse current-day insurance products on the individual markets across the states. Insurance is regulated at the state level, and each state has an insurance commissioner, an office that approves, oversees, and regulates all types of insurance, including health insurance. The ACA imposed a due date of July 2010, which was only four months after the bill was signed into law. So there was a mad scramble to put together a team and a plan to stand up a portal at the federal level and connect with state-level health insurance individual market products.

The immediate project became the first smaller scale version of HealthCare.gov. It was a tremendous feat in itself to get the first version up in four months, leveraging sources of information from commercial companies that worked with existing online brokers and insurers to deliver information about the health insurance products to various websites to support consumer shopping and agent/broker-assisted shopping. By July 2010, HealthCare.gov connected with these sources of data, aggregating and presenting the information in a uniform fashion much like if you were to type your travel itinerary into an online travel site and get options that fit or were close to the itinerary you specified.

This first version of HealthCare.gov would allow users to peruse, but in order to continue the process, they would select a product and then be redirected to the actual site or contact to apply for health-care coverage and go through the underwriting process in accordance with the pre-ACA process. Submitting it online did not automatically provide a decision on whether the individual was covered. In October 2013, this online application process for health-care coverage was significantly more complex given that the application had to adjudicate for a range of requirements including eligibility determination for Medicaid, CHIP, and/or APTCs.

The level of complexity and real-time delivery of accurate information for consumers to make choices for the future of HealthCare.gov was not unlike what took place in the airline industry. It used to be that airline tickets were handwritten on paper and there was a central booking system to track how many seats were sold on every plane. A very archaic system was used to figure the fare on a given date, flying routes, travel days and dates, and the number of layovers to a trip. With the advent of Travelocity, Expedia, and other online travel sites, all that pricing and information has to be available in real time. The airline industry took several years to really automate that process, so that now, no matter what ticket is sold through what channel, it's pretty much organized and kept track of centrally for most airlines.

Similarly, the online retailer, Amazon, may have a relatively easy-to-use, streamlined site for shoppers today, but it has evolved from where it began—and that took many years and certainly continues to evolve. Expectations for HealthCare.gov in 2013 to represent the optimal state of the health insurance industry—expectations that within three short years lacking detailed policies that were published on time, reengineering the business process of how insurance products were developed and compliant with the ACA essential health benefits requirements, reviewed by both state-level insurance commissioners and the federal regulators, and providing for guaranteed issuance would all be fully optimized and totally evolved on day one—were a tall order to fill. The continuing irony I observe in the IT industry is the notion that when you have an inefficient process without technology or with old technology, adding new technology to the equation automatically improves the process regardless of whether the inefficiencies could be addressed by technology changes. So we have the expectation that starting with a non-optimized health insurance product and sales model in 2010, by 2013 HealthCare. gov and its technologies will overcome all the problems for potentially twenty-plus million people in their selection and enrollment in health insurance products.

CHAPTER 5

DON'T BE A SHEEP

In all of my experiences participating in leadership, management, or executive-level training opportunities, there was always a portion that was devoted to the concepts of taking risks, not being afraid to fail, failing early and often, and so on. All were really to say that in order to be an effective leader, somewhere along the way you will face situations where there will naturally be some level of risk taking, either through your own actions or because you are responsible and accountable for the actions of your organization. How much risk can be taken and how much forgiveness is given for failed risk taking is highly dependent on the person you report to, the higher-up chain of command, and the overall culture of your organization.

In my twenty-one years at CMS, the culture was risk averse. Risk taking in general was foolish—even career ending. In some ways, being risk averse is understandable given that CMS is a highly complex organization that administers many different facets of health-care programs that touch the lives of more than a hundred million people in the United States. No one wants to adversely affect millions of people with poor decision making and unnecessary risk taking.

My perspective on risk taking at CMS developed from observing that nearly every year there was some major challenge levied on the agency, whether it was Medicare, Medicaid, CHIP, or the Insurance Marketplace program. Nearly every new initiative started on top of numerous other initiatives that launched previously, some taking multiple years to implement. Priorities were constantly being rebalanced, and resources were hardly ever adequate to support everything CMS was given to execute, not to mention the very typical and usual constraint of never having enough time to implement and stabilize new initiatives before the next disruption occurred. That all continued to happen while each political cycle made its course changes and adjustments amid previously established course changes in health care and health-care policies.

While most executives in CMS are conservative when it comes to taking risks, living under those circumstances creates tremendous opportunities for change, especially if the agency as a whole wants to be able to keep pace with the expectation that they will continuously implement new policies and regulations rather than sinking under the weight of it all.

In my experience at CMS, in certain situations, it was actually more prudent to do something different even if it was perceived as higher risk. Since CMS is charged with implementing new programs that are meant to transform the health-care landscape in the United States, it's difficult to achieve significant transformation without adopting new ways of thinking, planning, and executing rather than defaulting to what some refer to as a "paving over cow paths" approach to solving problems.

It is so much easier to just do what you've done before, especially if that requires the same process and similar outcomes. It is so much easier to budget the way you've always done it, contract the way you've always done it, and hire talent the way you've always done it—because organizations strive to optimize their administrative processes to do more with less and to become more efficient on behalf of the agency, right? People who work in IT also often revert to what has been done as the default approach to solving every existing and new problem, and then all the processes begin to have a tough time distinguishing between types of problems and situations that may require a different approach.

In this kind of environment, it is too easy to just go along like a sheep. Accepting the status quo can translate to a great disservice to the very people who are depending on you to implement programs effectively on their behalf.

Let me present that in a way that might hit closer to home. Just think about a time when you have to be an advocate for somebody close to you. Maybe you find out a loved one has a life-threatening illness and now you're left to make decisions for them. Are you just going to go along with what you're being told or are you going to try to educate yourself and be more proactive in finding them the best care? When it's closer to home, regarding a personal relationship with a named individual, it's easier to understand what it means to be an advocate.

> ACCEPTING THE STATUS QUO CAN TRANSLATE TO A GREAT DISSERVICE TO THE VERY PEOPLE WHO ARE DEPENDING ON YOU TO IMPLEMENT PROGRAMS EFFECTIVELY ON THEIR BEHALF.

Sometimes the sheer size and scale of a challenge can obfuscate a problem and cause people to resort to their default, sheep-like ways and just apply the same solution. Meanwhile, size and scale should be the key indicators that inform why the solution that works for, say, one million people doesn't work well for ten million people. HealthCare.gov was certainly problematic at launch for hundreds of thousands of users who were trying to register to create an account and subsequently move through the next steps of enrolling in a QHP, but the poor experience was not solely due to technical capacity and software quality issues. Rather, the technical capacity and software quality issues were a result of not fully understanding the size, scale, magnitude, complexity level, and the amount time needed to effectuate changes dictated by policy to transform how health insurance products were developed, approved, and sold on the Insurance Marketplaces.

That lack of awareness and inability to properly frame the expectations for how much change could be achieved in the prescribed time frame distorted the perceptions that problems such as technical capacity and software quality issues, which are inherent risks to any size IT project, are nothing that policy people need worry about because they are not interdependent. This false belief that the time IT needs to build, test, and deploy software and deliver adequate capacities is independent of policy and requirements was perpetuated throughout the agencies and departments as everyone just moved along at their respective pace like a herd of sheep. This recurring problem of policy development taking its twists and turns trying to dodge politics, bad press, and knowing that the maneuvering and indecision burns through much-needed time still plays out in a synthetic world where there's always time to hedge and change policy as needed, all the while staying ignorant about the eventual consequences of running out of time.

The press, media, critics, and every person who has an opinion about technology also behave like sheep when a government IT project has issues. They hear the results of what happens when there is too little time to turn requirements into code and focus only on the IT aspects of the project, not on the whole story. In a world of twenty-four-hour news cycles and competition to grab eyeballs, who really takes the time to try and understand the entire story before they write about it?

A LONELY VOICE

When a group comes together to try to come up with a strategy and a set of tactics to implement policy, it must be viewed through a very clear lens.

As an individual in such a group, you really have to ask: "Is this like anything I've ever seen before?" If you don't recognize it or understand it, instead of fearing it and just stepping back to see what others do, you must drive yourself to acquire the right knowledge and open up the thought processes to figure out the appropriate way to solve the situation.

In some situations, the problem is not even as complex as trying to determine the best way to implement policy. Sometimes it's the sheer march of time that cannot be changed. Too often, people lose sight of that fact. They'd rather be part of the crowd that waits for something to happen than be the one voice that says, "We're running out of time and we're headed for trouble."

That was a key discussion during the HealthCare.gov rollout. With only one or two lonely voices speculating about the prospect of time running out, and the consequences of eating up what little time there just wasn't an appetite for discussing delays or an alternate rollout strategy. Without more voices representing the technical and operational perspectives, there wasn't an opportunity to meaningfully evaluate the immediate correlating impacts to IT and operations resulting from shifts in policy positions. The constant policy wrangling and hesitation contributed to real consequences that, at the time, was not obvious to everyone but certainly by rollout time, it no longer mattered because all hands and eyes focused on the technology. That's not revolutionary thinking; that's the basics for any project.

DON'T RUN WITH THE PACK

When politics—especially politicians—are involved, the situation becomes even more difficult, because decisions tend to sway with the winds of popularity and polls. They're constantly swaying with their so-called base, which in reality could represent a very narrow distribution of the overall public being served.

At the micro level, that can be as discreet as a technical person making some design and implementation choices, or it may be someone making priority decisions about the logical order from a user-experience perspective of which policies to implement. At the macro level, it's the politics involved in ensuring there's enough support for a given piece of legislation or a particular political objective, focusing only on the so-called win and not its implications.

Either way, it's crucial not to just go along with the pack, in part because the pack might be doing something inherently obscene or wrong. Going along to get along is not the answer, especially if you're trying to solve a problem on behalf of other people. Saying "yes" to everyone instead of taking the unpopular stance of saying "no" can make a pending bad situation even worse.

Most would say that HealthCare.gov was an example of a failure to launch, but that's a gross mischaracterization. If there had been nothing there when "HealthCare.gov" was typed into the browser address bar on October 1, 2013, that would be a failure to launch. Over a thousand federal staff and contractors did everything possible within the time frame and resources given to deliver an MVP on day one so that there would not be a failure to launch—so that something was stood up as a starting point. Then the project would switch to operations mode and we could focus on fixes that would improve the site's performance and do the job of getting more people enrolled.

There were numerous occasions where the toxic political environment, vacillating policy decisions, lack of clear direction, and missteps by feds and contractors made it extremely difficult to determine what the priorities were. In such situations, instead of just going along and waiting for answers to come from above, you must have the courage to ask really tough questions and demand answers. If you are not given answers or directions that assist in the ability to make meaningful progress, then you must make the best call you can with the best available information to advance the project.

Sometimes the discussion around the development and delivery of an MVP with all the constraints applied implies that we live in a rational and reasonable world. Reality and experience says that once you set a target, you must adapt and change on a continuous basis in order to adjust for the irrational and illogical things that happen, but still deliver something that allows the program to launch rather than be completely dead on arrival.

NO GOOD DEED GOES UNPUNISHED

I had learned resourcefulness and true critical thinking in the Navy, and early in my career with the HCFA, I was informed that I was a little too inquisitive. I often tried to volunteer or ask questions such as "Why can't we do these things a little differently?" until my supervisor at the time told me, "Henry, just remember, no good deed goes unpunished." Basically, he was trying to tell me that it was safer not to put myself out there, or I would forever be tagged for the difficult tasks. Back then, I didn't realize that getting in the thick of things to really figure out how to solve problems actually suited my personality.

For some time after that, I was like many other people—I didn't really ask any questions because it was uncomfortable to do so. I often didn't feel that I had really understood the subject matter well enough.

When someone is new in a role, it takes time to "grow legs," so to speak. But you have to take a chance, because waiting for someone to come put their arm around you and sanction that it's okay for you to make mistakes is not going to happen.

In a recent conference, I recall someone saying the problem with the world today is that people don't fail enough. Learning occurs in failure. But in order to fail, you have to take a chance. If you work in an environment that doesn't encourage taking risks, how are you ever going to learn? You have to take it upon yourself to do so— even if you're in the environment of public service, which is not very encouraging of taking calculated risks.

Have the courage to ask questions and raise issues. Even when in a situation where "no" is unpopular, go back and look at your own contribution to the whole. If you build your character and career around self-preservation, then you miss out on the opportunities to build instincts, confidence, and self-awareness that comes with risk taking. You fail to see how you can actually learn from sticking your neck out by, say, asking a question that causes other people to chuckle or whisper under their breath.

When you have the courage not to follow blindly along, not to be a sheep, and when you can overcome the immediate embarrassment of any situation you find yourself in, you build a work character that becomes more and more resilient. With that confidence, you can solve more problems and truly embrace the implications for the millions of people who are impacted by the decisions you're involved in. But you may never arrive at the realization that what you do is that important if you don't start by driving yourself to take a chance.

IT'S ABOUT PERSISTENCE

One of the reasons HealthCare.gov had such a huge, problematic rollout was that no one stakeholder would give anything up. Everybody wanted everything, and they fought tooth and nail to keep it all. I was in the background trying to shepherd everything and help determine an absolute MVP where there was mostly take and no give. In the end, time the becomes the biggest factor in determining which priority requirements is in the MVP .

My approach to solving problems is to go to whatever end needed to find a resolution. If you lock the front door on me, I'm going to try to go to the backdoor. If you lock the backdoor, I'm going to try to climb through the window. If you lock all the windows, I'm going to try to dig a hole and tunnel in. It's about persistence. Not persistence because you need to have your way, although I'm sure that's the way persistence is often perceived, but rather, persistence on behalf of those people who are nameless.

If you're in a situation where you find different teams are myopically working within their own path of least resistance in order to preserve their own agendas when they are supposed to cohesively deliver an integrated product, you have to find a way to help the different teams focus on a collective set of priorities rather than obsess over their own. This can be extremely difficult especially if the teams individually report to different management teams. Everyone declares they are following the directive of their respective managers and when you approach the different managers to create cooperation from the top down, the reaction often is defensive rather than collegial. This is a situation where you have to "tunnel" in by any means, such as looking for proxies, third parties that can broker productive conversations, and yes, even barter and trade tactics. When it comes down to convincing people to do the right thing, such as working together to deliver an integrated product and experience for the public, you are now operating at the "relationship" level, which then really tests your abilities to move people through influence and appealing to their ideals while tactfully balancing persistence, sense of urgency, and resourcefulness with mountains of patience.

When that happens, you really are going back to basics.

CHAPTER 6

LESS-THAN-DESIRABLE OPTIONS? GO BACK TO THE BASICS

There are some very good workshops and management classes for senior-grade federal employees. They're very expensive, and it's time consuming to go through them, especially for someone with a busy schedule. But they're well worth the investment, because they take you back to the basics—the ideals of democracy, the decency that is within all of us, and how our history and ideals, however imperfect, still serve as a shining light to those who aspire beyond who they are today, and to remember that no matter where we come from, we all have a hand in shaping our collective future. The programs train through group activities and a humanities approach to topics—such as personal goals that you're going to try to achieve using what you learned in the course and how to deal with challenges such as making public policy decisions in very critical circumstances.

While the courses are very close to being experiential, they're still a little shy of reality. Most training is like that. The exercises simulate circumstances or case studies where there is a clear right choice and a clear wrong choice, when in the real world that's rarely the case. By training only for the clear right or wrong, you're not really prepared for real-world situations such as being in a time crunch on a very high complexity program where you're repeatedly presented with multiple options, none of which are clearly more optimal. And inevitably, with many training and educational environments, there are good or right answers—as compared to circumstances in the real world where the best answer depends on the available information. Sometimes it is a luxury to be able to choose between a good and a bad answer or option.

When you're working on a project where all the options seem pretty dismal, you still must be able to sort through all the information and make a decision. In order to make a decision, you have to choose the best possible path. You have to be able to embrace every situation and find your way, even if it's not so clear.

DOING WHAT'S DOABLE WITH THE BEST AVAILABLE INFORMATION

After the HealthCare.gov rollout, a lot of folks descended on the scene, saying, "We would never have done it this way." But they provided that opinion, particularly about the technology, without knowing the thousands of decisions that had to be made and whether the information available for making decisions was good or bad. Because when making a set of cascading decisions while barreling toward a specified date, the decisions are always made based on the best available information at the time.

In January of 2015, the Department of Health and Human Services' Office of the Inspector General (OIG) published a report titled, "Federal Marketplace: Inadequacies in Contract Planning and Procurement." In summary, the OIG asserted that CMS did not develop an overarching acquisition strategy and whatever had been done was inadequate and there were missed opportunities to leverage available acquisition tools. The OIG team that produced the report met with several of the CMS leads on the Insurance Marketplace program in 2014 for the entrance meeting, a kick-off of sorts.[2] The OIG team was very professional and cordial in the way they conducted the meeting and we jumped right into discussions on what were some of the factual elements that helped explain the acquisition strategy we had used throughout the preceding years leading up to the launch of HealthCare.gov. I was very frank in sharing my perspective on why the acquisition strategy was flawed, as the OIG team very adeptly pointed out. There was no disagreement but I provided what I believed to be an extremely salient point that is a crucial predecessor to realistically plan and execute a viable acquisition strategy. From the time I formally joined OCIIO in July of 2010 as the CIO and over the next eighteen months, we lived in one of the most budget challenged situations I ever encountered working in government. So much uncertainty swirled about regarding how much funding we actually could depend on for IT and business contracts, and that uncertainty severely constrained the ability to logically, and smartly plan and execute the acquisition strategy. I can only speak to what

---

2   "Federal Marketplace: Inadequacies in Contract Planning and Procurement,"
     Office of the Inspector General, U.S. Department of Health & Human Services,
     January 20, 2015, https://oig.hhs.gov/oei/reports/oei-03-14-00230.asp

I was able to control, which were the six IT contracts that received formal review by our Office of Acquisition and Grants Management. While those contracts received the greatest scrutiny, they were also the ones that were the source of much debate about how much budget we really, really needed to get to October 1st and beyond. The simple explanation for why we had a poor acquisition strategy is that without certainty in budget and funding levels, how can you reasonably plan and execute contracting for IT and services when you don't know how much you have in the bank? If funding is erratic and unstable for the first eighteen months of a program, how sound of an acquisition strategy can you really have? And if you have an acquisition strategy but it's unfunded, how can you execute it?

DECISIONS BASED ON IMPACT

When the situation you're dealing with is less than optimal, making decisions begins by understanding that in many cases, there is no right or wrong. There are only degrees of impact on end users related to the decision that is made.

One of the most difficult questions to answer was: What is absolutely critical to launch the Insurance Marketplace program? With so much stakeholder input and influence, multiple business units—each with their own sense of priorities and other critical factors such as budget, contracting, and HR—locked down the initial MVP. Through additional incremental builds, the business units added required features and functionality which resulted in a brutal exercise in which you never get to a final answer.

Do you sacrifice minimum functionality that allows the program to start or do you try to satisfy every requirement in hopes that a miracle will happen and all the realities of lack of time, resources, and clarity somehow all magically work themselves out? This is the example of choosing the lesser of two evils—fail to deliver some features and a "world class" user experience or fail completely? This is the reality you have to embrace so you can clearly understand the relative impact between something bad and something beyond really bad.

In most real-world situations where the complexities of what you are trying to accomplish receive none of the necessary resources and time, you have to be able to choose options that may make you a very unpopular person, but still produce some level of progress toward an intended outcome. Tough decisions must be made when everybody wants everything and you're left with the prospect of determining what's doable in the amount of time you have. Someone is going to be unhappy in the process, so decisions must be based on the greater good.

Making tough decisions often comes down to "throwing everything out of the airplane" and leaving only those pieces of the plane that are needed to keep it aloft. With HealthCare.gov, since the launch date was immovable, we had to launch with whatever we had and then fix that as we went along.

If you think about the realities of what goes into deciding the launch of anything, try a slightly different context—consumer electronics. Products coming out of the tech industry launch with numerous bugs, but that doesn't stop the world's largest makers of consumer technology. They decide when the

> **TOUGH DECISIONS MUST BE MADE WHEN EVERYBODY WANTS EVERYTHING AND YOU'RE LEFT WITH THE PROSPECT OF DETERMINING WHAT'S DOABLE IN THE AMOUNT OF TIME YOU HAVE.**

software and hardware is good enough to be used and push it out, then fix the bugs after the fact. Granted, this is not an apples-to apples comparison since building and launching an online application to enroll in health-care coverage is a bit more complex with much greater emphasis on protecting people's personal information. However, since building national scale health IT systems often gets compared to consumer apps and online retail transactions, let's take a closer look at what really happens with launches of consumer tech products, such as some smart phones and their batteries, security vulnerabilities discovered after launch such as with Internet of Things (IOT) devices, autonomous vehicles, and more. My point is, debating about what should have been done in IT implementations is highly subjective and unproductive. The presumption that there's some perfected state for any technology distracts and distorts efforts to address the real issues.

CHAPTER 7

TRUST YOURSELF

In June 2010, the OMB, which is part of the White House, sponsored a kickoff meeting between the IRS and HHS. I represented OCIIO on the technology side. The White House dispatched bioethicist and oncologist Ezekiel Emanuel. He wanted to ensure that we understood that whatever we were going to build, which would launch a few years down the road, was going to provide for what he called a "world-class experience" in shopping for health insurance online. That was a tall order, and a squishy definition, since shopping for health insurance online with guaranteed issuance, real-time adjudication of eligibility for APTCs, Medicaid, and/or CHIP programs, and ending with enrollments in the appropriate and consumer-selected coverages did not exist anywhere in the United States at that time.

While we all understood the intent behind Mr. Emanuel's declaration and the spirit and intent of the ACA, we also knew the ACA was intended to disrupt the health insurance markets with tremendous policy and business process changes. Under the ACA, the mountain of change in developing and regulating health insurance products across federal agencies, state agencies, and insurance companies would be where the real challenges were, meaning all stakeholders had to understand what the policy changes meant in real, operational terms such as functioning systems that processed data as intended by the requirements of the law.

All of the career federal staff in the room knew that this tall order would be extremely difficult to execute along what would be an even more unstable and shorter time frame than any of us imagined. But we were there for a reason. Those of us who had been in the thick of major health-care program rollouts and lived through the twenty-four seven operational efforts to stabilize a new program knew that our respective jobs were to do whatever was necessary to go live by October 1, 2013, even if it was something less than a "world-class experience."

We were at the precipice of an effort to significantly change the current health-care landscape. While daunting to think about achieving such a dramatic transformation in just a few years, what made it so much more difficult was the number of stakeholders involved, all of which also had to change to some great degree. That included insurance companies, insurance industry associations, state insurance commissioners, insurance agents and brokers, online insurance brokers, state Medicaid and CHIP programs, state and county eligibility caseworkers, SSA, IRS, Treasury, DHS, DoD, VA, OPM, CMS, Peace Corps, Standards Development Organizations, and all the IT vendors, service providers, and contractors that support these organizations. And they all needed information to flow from the policies and regulations developed by the federal government—so that they could then translate to the requirements that helped them implement the changes introduced by the ACA. Very few people realized that the lack of clarity on policies and lack of decisions being made about policies and when to release them didn't just "hog-tie" the federal government and impede the ability to make progress; that situation was magnified as other stakeholders that needed clarity on the requirements became even further behind.

When you recognize how dire a situation is and that there aren't any "good" options to choose, you can't be paralyzed by the situation. What you can do is see past the nonsense and use your experience and instincts that have been developed by years of trial by fire. Control what you can and make decisions that produce some forward momentum toward the goal. Trust yourself to mitigate high-risk situations by thinking very clearly about what you can do in the absence of solid requirements. That includes seeing past all the chaos from political theatrics and wrangling that wastes even more time that you can't control because that mess lives in a political dimension all on its own. While quite real in terms of political survival, in our situation, it was completely detached from the reality of how to make the program work in some fashion on day one.

When you're involved in a project that's surrounded by turmoil, you must trust your instincts. You must trust in what you know and your attitude toward learning and adapting. Because in such situations, turmoil becomes a natural part of how every day unfolds, and you must be able to separate your internal feelings from it—even when some of that turmoil directly involves you. If you don't trust yourself and how to get things done in that hazardous environment, you can't allow the swirling to consume you or your team. If nothing else, you have to be the anchor and the beacon, staying steadfast while giving hope that there are some still focused on getting to day one and on exactly what has to be done to stand up a range of systems that real people will use to enroll and access health care.

When a major initiative starts off like this with artificially high expectations, how do you survive the reality that ensues when you know it's such a difficult undertaking? For instance, the expectation that a new website for purchasing health insurance online will be a world-class experience similar to the mature Amazon model is, at best, unclear and ambiguous in terms of the critical aspects of designing, architecting, and engineering that experience from scratch. So you must understand and appreciate what exactly is at hand to deliver an MVP and not get lost in chasing the lofty expectations or be consumed by the lack of good options. You have to remain calm and take the best available information each day and continuously adapt the changes while continuing along the path of constructing what the fundamental pieces of technology are that, when coupled together like Lego blocks, produce the capabilities to provide some ability to enroll online—even though that enrollment on day one will not necessarily be instantaneous and produce a similar user experience as Amazon, especially given that providing and maintaining a good user experience is an ongoing, evolving process that takes many years.

DEFINING SUCCESS IN GOVERNMENT ENDEAVORS

I've taken my fair share of courses where "critical success factors" or "key performance indicators" are discussed as necessary to defining success in organizational endeavors to deliver an expected outcome. Similarly, in many of the projects I've worked on there have been lofty discussions of what performance indicators would be collected to gauge the success of the project. These are noble gestures that are not bad things to want as part of your project, but in government projects, coming up with measures of success is not that straightforward. Over the years, I've heard so many attempts at putting government projects side by side with private sector projects, and I have conceded that there are better practices to be learned from the private sector. But "better" presumes the comparisons are apples to apples.

There are so many things in an organized and enlightened society that are inherently governmental, such as a national military force, the judiciary, food safety, law enforcement, social security, and health-care programs for the elderly, disabled, veterans, and many more. It wouldn't be impossible for a private company to step in and run one of these inherently governmental functions, but the underlying motivation would be drastically different. Private sector companies' motivations and decision-making processes are closely tied to generating revenue to cover expenses, and generate profit and growth. The private sector company's success is measured by revenue, profit, and ability to meet or exceed shareholder expectations, while the government is measured by how well it serves the people, how well it provides for the health and safety of its population, and so on. And how well it performs is often measured by the trust and confidence of its people.

Don't get me wrong—that does not mean everything works as intended for public or private organizations. In comparing public and private sector big projects, consider everything rather than just selected components. Projects such as HealthCare.gov took years of struggle to launch and then years for the program to stabilize and improve how the systems are managed in an operational context. In that regard, it is similar to major projects in the private sector. Amazon, Google, and Facebook did not launch in the condition in which they serve customers today. And if they survive, in a few short years the user experience may be different than it is today.

Defining success for HealthCare.gov, then, was launching the MVP on October 1, 2013, regardless of what other conditions existed. In the private sector, if the MVP was not up to shape and would impact revenue, profits, valuation, reputation, and branding, it would be highly likely that someone would step on the brakes and reassess. For HealthCare.gov, the political train started forty-two months prior. During that time, thousands of stakeholders were onboarded, and the momentum that developed was a key factor in not being able to do anything other than launch. So an MVP in the private sector does not equal an MVP in the public sector, because success is measured on different terms and defined by a very different and diverse universe of stakeholders. Still, many "experts" immediately came up with their versions of what happened and how a rollout like HealthCare.gov would never happen in the private world. Consider all the parts of the health insurance world that had to change or adapt to the policies and requirements under the ACA and how stakeholders in that world needed clear requirements and guidance so that they could deliver what they needed for a functional Marketplace. In the private sector, would teams and their management withhold information from suppliers but still hold everyone to the same timeline and expect delivery of each project?

Success is also often defined by the sense of urgency, or even the lack of relative urgency, depending on whether you are waiting on someone else or they are waiting on you. Just look at the House of Representatives and its two-year election cycles. The day after a congressperson is elected, that person and their staff are already calculating and planning on getting reelected. The Senate moves at a slightly more leisurely pace, because its reelection cycle is six years. The presidency, of course, operates in between the two. Because of the rightfully intentional differences in the cycles, the unintended effect shows up in how it's so difficult for government to commit to anything that's truly long term. There are many superficial efforts to address longer term needs such as improving the nation's infrastructure, immigration laws, removing bias in the criminal justice system, health care for all, and a tax system that doesn't feel like it's rigged. Perhaps this is more of a recent phenomenon, where the unintended effects of professional politicians running on two, four, and six-year hamster wheels is that all that really matters is getting reelected and not working together to legislate for the future of the nation and its people. No one wants to make those long-view promises; they want to make things sound more immediate. Between fiscal years 1977 and 2015, Congress only managed to pass the twelve regular appropriation bills on time in four of the thirty-eight years. Seems like that measure of success can be improved.[3]

The similarities in behavior about goals and objectives between the public and private sectors is something that the general public often misses. When national-scale programs like the Insurance Marketplaces/HealthCare.gov are implemented, there's a very misguided notion that success is rather instantaneous, when these kinds of programs actually take decades to mature. Have Medicare, Medicaid, and the health insurance industry as a whole been spectacularly successful? The systems, data, and processes that support the programs are continuously challenged to keep up with policy changes, growth in volume, and ability to interoperate with other health-care systems and data. With all of that in motion, how do you determine success and failure of such a complex operation, with some number of individuals experiencing less-than-optimal service? Complex programs take decades to stabilize and improve. And then they continue to evolve as the world changes.

3   Carl L. Moravitz, "Nuts and Bolts on the Congressional Budget Process," presentation to the Bureau of the Fiscal Treasury, US Department of the Treasury, Aug. 17, 2015, accessed April 5, 2018, https://fiscal.treasury.gov/fstraining/events/17_Congressional_Budget_Process.pdf.

Understanding and appreciating the realities of what motivates public and non-public institutions and their endeavors is not all you need to know to navigate the twists and turns of numerous internal and external critics who have an opinion on what success is supposed to look like. While some of those opinions can be helpful, it's up to you to filter out the ones that are not. That means the knowledge and instincts you've gained from years of firsthand experiences must give you the confidence and ability to distinguish what is immediately important while still balancing what can be deferred. To make progress, you must trust your awareness of the hard and soft boundaries in which you operate, and in time-compressed, chaotic situations, choose absolutely the most critical priorities that will deliver the MVP.

THE END RESULT—A MIRROR OF THE COLLECTIVE

An amazing number of people don't realize that systems automate, on a very large scale, what humans manually perform or aspire to achieve. How well these systems perform for those that they serve depends on the collective abilities of the humans who worked on designing and building the system. In other words, how well systems perform (how technology is applied) represents the collective ability (or inability) of the people who worked on the system to communicate and coordinate the outcome.

I've been approached by many people from the tech industry and academia, students and journalists, staff from the US Digital Service, and other walks of life asking questions that reveal that they presume everyone who works on a given project is motivated to share information in an open and transparent manner and that everyone moves at the same level of urgency. Given that presumption, where everyone knows what to do, how to do it, and when to do it, I would also question why HealthCare.gov rolled out the way it did. Since people were obviously working together, the problems must have been the quality of work, quality of the technology and its implementation, and poor management and decision-making processes.

But that was not the case. It was a politically toxic environment that involved working across many organizational boundaries and cultures coupled with the lack of willingness to share information openly and in a timely manner. That explains why certain decisions were made, such as why we launched knowing there would be problems. Technology notwithstanding, just consider the broader issues that loom over every project involving multiple teams from multiple organizations trying to make progress under similar conditions. Getting everyone pointed in the same direction with the same level of urgency, equal understanding, and acceptance of the priorities is a realistic and consistent set of threats to teams that are trying to make progress toward an objective.

When working on this kind of project with so many stakeholder teams that have multiple perspectives and priorities—all converging in the delivery of a unified product consumers could use—can sometimes make the user experience seem secondary to all the teams trying to get their requirements implemented. I think it's fair to say that "a good user experience" isn't necessarily a unique requirement that needs to be declared each and every time there's a need to build some interface that a user/person would interact with, but there has to be a balance between absolute necessity and what is nice to have. Designing the user experience when you are building a government system requires understanding what a given user type expects and prefers with requirements that are imposed by federal laws and regulations, as these govern how security and privacy is implemented in a federal information system. Between the frame of reference of the actual user and the frame of reference that designers/developers operate under as they adhere to a set of policies, business rules, and requirements governing the interaction with the user, the goal is to still provide a user experience that is acceptable while still maintaining the best possible security posture and abilities to protect sensitive data.

In the HealthCare.gov context, there was a federal requirement to authenticate all users who access a federal information system. Before an application for enrollment is created, users have to first register and create an account choosing a user ID and password, which is then authenticated through an identity management system and a remote identity proofing service. This was not well received by many users, and it was seen as overly burdensome. That mandatory step in the enrollment process was seen as a significant detractor from a good user experience, aside from having its own rollout issues.

So often in efforts to design user experiences for the general public, imposing what seems to be cumbersome and unnecessary security precautions isn't just a compliance exercise to dogmatically follow laws and regulations. Designing a user experience is not just a point-in-time exercise. It requires taking a comprehensive view of what the full lifecycle requirements are for initially engaging the user, supporting their needs to update and change information, and imposing what may seem to be cumbersome security measures but in actuality is done to protect the user from having their data compromised as well as protecting other user's data. Prevention measures to protect people's online accounts starts with authenticating the user's identity through simple countermeasures. These include asking questions that only the actual user would know the answers to, texting a code to your smartphone to enter during login, and managing your role and what you have access to.

The initial result of the implementation of HealthCare.gov may seem to be a scramble of whatever requirements we were able to cram by day one, and it may be hard to convince anyone that there was a constant, conscious effort to manage the trade-offs between user experience, the absolute necessary requirements, and the daily dynamics of what would be nice to have that can be deferred to a later date than day one. The outcome indeed represents how the collective teams and people were able to jointly deliver, and it took a tremendous amount of stamina and resilience to continuously rebalance what was necessary with what could be deferred.

NO SINGLE RAINDROP CAUSES THE FLOOD

When it comes to information technology, it's important to have a blueprint for what you want to build. A "blueprint" is a loosely used term in the practice of an EA program. It can consist of conceptual architecture diagrams, business process models, high-level data flows, major interfaces and interactions, and, of course, many of the above come in the form of PowerPoint slides—the default, and every person's architecture tool. All such documents can define a destination and serve as a road map to get to some desired end state or series of end states. The Winchester Mystery House in San Jose is a good example of what happens without such a road map. Without having and following a set of objectives, you end up with randomness, like the stairwells that go nowhere in that house. Just like Lady Winchester, who was driven on some level by thought processes that were not rational, people often make decisions that are not based on rational reasoning when it comes to choosing how to apply technology.

A road map is not a guarantee that a given project will be inoculated from excessive visitation of priorities. The demand to entertain every possible requirement or a loss of focus on how time affects how much can be done can turn a logical and fairly linear journey along a path of least resistance into a road trip from hell where you repeatedly revisit places you've already been. Individuals and teams that cause the revisit effect, many times due to lack of clear and timely requirements, often force everyone to back up to a previous start point or create last-minute changes in policies. That creates mounting risk just from the amount of lost time. With any project of scale, it isn't about one group of people who have a collective, coordinated set of requirements. It's about multiple teams working in parallel. Unfortunately, what often happens is that all those teams expect to be treated with equal priority, because no single raindrop believes it is the cause of the flood.

A lot of project teams are like that. They're very passionate. They want to execute based on their swim lane and what they want to get done. And considering that every other team is feeling the same way, the default slogan tends to be: "That's not my job. My job is to execute in the swim lane I am in, to report only to certain people, and to get only these objectives done."

The problem is, if a dozen teams have that same mindset, it can really strain the process. When no one is willing to give up anything in terms of what they need to get done, someone has to step up and be the mediator to get the right combination of priorities executed.

Sometimes that means being the pragmatic soul who stands up and says, "Okay, I get what you want to do. I'm not going to tell you that you can't have what you want. I'll try to get you what you want, but just be aware that constraints such as time, resources, and complexity will dictate how things will come out."

Often in complex endeavors where you have, and need, multiple teams that represent the range of domain expertise and disciplines, you might be disappointed if you expect the teams to be self-regulating and coordinated across domains and disciplines. This is why we have program offices, program managers, systems integrators (SIs), and general contractors to act as the "glue" and represent the collective consciousness so the outcomes are clear. Even if you have formally put in place or contracted for the program manager, program office, SI, and/or a general contractor, that does not absolve you of the responsibility and accountability for ensuring the coordination and integration across the teams is aligned with the intended outcomes—you still have to be vigilant.

So, trust how your decisions will lead to the desired outcome— an outcome that may be magnitudes away from success (even though success was not well defined) and that others may call a failure, but still gets you through the first day. You must know within yourself that, given the circumstances, what you've done is as good as it can be, and that it will get better beyond day one.

EFFECTIVE COMMUNICATION AND AUTHORITY

It's good to be passionate about a role in a project, but not so much that it compromises the ability to think collectively. The key is to think collectively, understand trade-offs, and communicate about those trade-offs.

In government, for example, policy people tend to be very passionate about the outcomes of their policy, and anything that appears as challenging them about that passion can be problematic—it's perceived as attacking the intent of the person. But the combination of everyone's intent must be accounted for simultaneously. It's impossible for everyone to go first at the same time.

Still, when communicating with people on projects, people who take pride in ownership, it can seem as if you're questioning their passion. That's when it becomes crucial to get them to think about more than just their own interests. They need to be made aware of what's going to happen if they don't give a little. And that doesn't happen by just dismissing their concerns or challenging their passion. Everyone must feel like their concerns are being accommodated. It can be a very fragile situation when folks perceive that they are being asked for their swim lane to take a back seat to others.

Effective communication is even more critical for people in leadership roles. People look to leaders during tough times as a gauge, as a barometer, to how bad a situation is—should they abandon ship, or should they continue to push forward? If a leader shows that the situation is survivable past day one, then others won't feel like everything is falling apart.

Many people who occupy positions of leadership exhibit rather superficial leadership qualities. Often it's because they ascended to a particular position of authority and leadership but just don't have the experience to exhibit the forcefulness they need to get things done. And much of the experience has to be rooted in the ability to take measured risks in choosing what may be better for the long term— and not be viewed as building and implementing something no one explicitly asked for. If you are looking at implementing a national-scale program that redefines the scope of the term "enterprise" because it's just that large and complex, there are very few people who have lived through those experiences and are able to apply forward what they learned.

There's an old saying that I often found to be appropriate in cases where leaders across government and the technology industry showed up to offer their services but ultimately had ulterior motives: "Lead, follow, or get out of the way." A lot of people in positions of leadership can't seem to get out of the way—in fact, they sometimes get more defensive when it seems that is what they need to do. In a fast-paced situation where things are not going well and you have to make some very tough choices, you don't have time to stroke the ego of an insecure leader. You basically have to get a little tough and let them know that they have a choice: "Lead, follow, or get out of the way."

My Navy experience taught me that you can delegate responsibility, but you can't delegate accountability. That is the key dimension of knowing yourself and setting that inner compass that you trust. When you've experienced a similar situation in which you've been able to drive people forward, then you can potentially use that as a basis for other situations.

And if you're going to trust yourself, you must "own it," both the good and the bad.

CHAPTER 8

"OWN IT"—THE GOOD AND THE BAD

Working on the ACA Insurance Marketplace program wasn't the first messy situation that I had been in. The Medicare prescription drug program (Part D) was also a major challenge, one in which no single person could possibly do everything right all the time. The launch of Part D was not without major issues. The major difference is that while it was President George W. Bush and the Republicans' major initiative, the Democrats did not go to the lengths that the Republicans have from 2010 to 2017, in still trying to re-legislate what their own branch of government has passed.

Part D had significant challenges with data issues, Medicare. gov availability issues, confusion from shifting an initial seven million FBDEs from prescription drug coverage through Medicaid to Medicare Part D coverage, all on a single day—January 1, 2006. All the issues were critical and had real impact on people's lives, and there was plenty of coverage by the media, and even lawsuits filed, but there wasn't a distorted amplification of the issues such as with HealthCare.gov.

The policy, technical, and operations teams from Medicare, Medicaid, state agencies, insurance companies, and the entire health-care industry all kept their heads down working toward launch and post-launch stabilization efforts. Even amid some major concerns that were conveyed from the political leadership, we remained calm and eventually worked through all the messy issues, which took more than a year. Everyone involved learned some significant lessons that would carry over to the HealthCare.gov effort. One core lesson was to remain calm and not become paralyzed by the pressure and complexity of the situation. That had to be done in order to think clearly through the problems and devise plans to fix them even when one might fix data issues for a million enrollments but not correct tens of thousands of records. That meant moving ahead for the greater good and then continuously working back down the residual problems.

PROVIDING TEAMS WITH A LEADERSHIP STYLE THAT IS STEADY AND FOCUSED PREVENTS THE LOSS OF MOTIVATION AND CONFIDENCE IN THE COLLECTIVE ABILITY TO RESOLVE PROBLEMS THAT MAY AT THE MOMENT SEEM INSURMOUNTABLE.

Remaining calm and continuing to make decisions to drive progress is key in motivating teams to shift from the shock of initial launch, which can have an overwhelming and nonstop onslaught of issues to fix, to immediately embracing the complex problems and dissecting them down to workable pieces. Providing teams with a leadership style that is steady and focused prevents the loss of motivation and confidence in the collective ability to resolve problems that may at the moment seem insurmountable. There's no time to duck for fear of being blamed for something bad happening.

Particularly in times where it would be easier to duck, you must do the opposite. You must stay and fight the good fight, because it isn't about you, it's about the people you serve, the people who count on you to make things work as they should on their behalf. Working on CMS programs is not about the faceless public. It's about the people in your family and community who ask for assistance in understanding insurance processes and Medicare, Medicaid, and Insurance Marketplace policies. Thinking about the impact on other's lives is what really keeps it real—that's what can keep you from running and hiding. Stand up and own all the good and bad so that you can proceed to do the real work rather than dwell on whether blame is correctly assigned.

Without embracing it all—the good and the bad—there is a tendency to focus superficially on whether you are going to get the blame. The sooner you can take that step, the sooner you can get to the next logical step in solving the problem. Learning and growth come from making mistakes. Constantly running away from blame and worrying about making mistakes never lets you get to that depth of understanding about what happened, and life becomes a constant escape from anything that seems bad.

NO ROOM FOR "ME" PERSONALITIES

Even though each individual's contributions on a large project team are subject to both positive and negative criticism—and sometimes it means facing the fact that a bad decision was made—there's no room for "me" personalities.

In the past, craftsmen, tradesmen, farmers, and the like were the entire system in and of themselves. They sourced their material, put in the labor, shaped and honed the product, and then brought it to market. In a postindustrial society, the highly industrialized division of labor for efficiency's sake created specialization. A giant machine could take a manufacturing process and break it into different components that people were individually responsible for, with all the components coming together in the end. We're still largely living in that postindustrial mindset of taking a larger problem and decomposing it into its parts, working on the parts individually, and then assembling them together when it makes logical sense to do so.

Even with some of the recent trends toward adopting agile approaches in software development arising, agile still requires someone to focus on the convergence or integration of the whole. Whether you're manufacturing widgets or developing software and then putting it together for an online enrollment system, it's about completely focusing on the delivery of that integrated solution. How well the individual tasks are being performed and completed contributes to an integrated, intended outcome but by themselves are not the centerpiece of the work. The integration is the centerpiece.

With HealthCare.gov, we knew that the policy and requirements would be released very late, so we became opportunistic and focused on being agile, using what was solid enough information to feed in to the early design and requirements engineering efforts. Whenever we had enough information on an increment of an epic or story, we'd do a sprint to see if we could define as much detail as possible. And while that's not necessarily aligned with the agile gods, it does try to adapt agile to a real-world circumstance in which you're trying to reclaim a lot of time, and you know that it's going to be a precious commodity as you get closer to the implementation date.

Agile by itself, however, would not have changed the outcome of the rollout. In fact, agile could have made things worse, and that would have been a much more serious situation. Think of it this way.

Your teams develop and test code based on what everyone thought was a complete story and/or epic, but it turns out that they are incomplete or have assumptions and requirements that are significantly changed months down the road. Then add to that situations where priorities and the sequencing of initiatives change—the development teams have to shift their focus and rearrange their build schedules.

Whether a project is agile or otherwise, the project needs a beacon—a person who has the knowledge, awareness, wherewithal, and ability to cross boundaries to get things done. Such a person must be someone who can see the ultimate end product, or at least an increment of it—someone who holds that vision and then drives everything toward it by working with one or more teams. That's the bottom line with any project: Who's keeping an eye on what needs to be delivered? That needs to be somebody who is willing to take responsibility across the board—with the project components and with multiple people.

A DISHEARTENING POV

In early September 2013, I brought a core team of my staff onsite at CGI's office in Herndon, Virginia working eighteen to twenty hours a day to ensure we would have an MVP by October 1st. From our past experiences, we already knew that while day one was critical, we also were prepared to immediately shift to a live, operational mode, and it was time to troubleshoot production issues while still continuing to make progress building the necessary pieces that were scheduled for post-day one delivery. Launching the centerpiece of ACA drew attention and curiosity around the world, which resulted in even more traffic to HealthCare.gov. As you can imagine, the atmosphere was intense and everyone was extremely stressed, but they maintained focus and composure—even as news trucks started camping out in the parking lot and journalists accosted staff as they entered or left the building. As the news cycles began to focus on the launch and away from the government shutdown that also commenced on October 1st, the pressure increased more and more each passing day. The entire team had to take bold steps to fix the highest priority problems such as errors preventing users to register and create accounts, and as the situation improved, we would then shift to the next set of issues. Given the mountain of issues our teams had to work with and through, it was truly a remarkable accomplishment to make it to day one, but from the outside looking in, it certainly wasn't perceived that way.

What made it even more challenging after the rollout was the painting of the façade that there was a rescue team which descended upon the situation and fix the problems in a little over sixty days. A major source of fuel for supporting the rescue narrative came in the form of a fourteen-page article published in *Time* magazine in March 2014, titled "Code Red: Inside the nightmare launch of HealthCare. gov and the team that figured out how to fix it." The article was written by a well-known and highly credible journalist, Steven Brill. The article was fairly comprehensive in summarizing the events that unfolded starting on October 17th, the day before the all-day van ride of the first crew that arrived to jump in and help. The story portrayed a group of very smart and successful people that sacrificed whatever was going on in their lives to perform this noble deed to make things right. All of the career federal employees and quite a few people on the contractor teams who read the article were scratching their heads wondering who contributed to the information used in the article other than the people in the inner circle. Most of us that lived the realities of the nightmare as expressed by the title of the article wondered how complete this story really was if it lacked our point-of-view and didn't capture the root causes that created the nightmare. It seemed clear at the time, at least for those that lived through the preceding years, that a better version of history was needed at the time to weather the storms. Todd Park, the federal government's CTO at the time, assisted in reaching out to the individuals that jumped in to help and continued to recruit more and more "volunteers" to bring their talent in to the mix to turn things around.

Speaking on behalf of the people who were there that scrambled to make the launch date and had already shifted to fixing the issues, continuing to build remaining pieces, and to improve the performance of the systems, the notion that there was a rescue team that came to fix what was so darn obvious to any tech professional was insulting at best. It's not that we were thin-skinned and took personal offense to a story that exaggerated the role of those that came to help, and that without that help, we all would have been doomed. It's more about integrity, honesty, respect for the truth, and the disappointment that yet another story was told focusing on technology as the culprit and perpetuating the myth that projects always fail because of issues related solely to technology.

So think about it: This program was about major change in the way people accessed affordable health insurance across the nation. Given the stories of how big a disaster the rollout was, was it really even feasible that such a mess could be turned around in a little over sixty days as the story would have you believe? The truth is that there were massive issues to fix and *everyone* involved was doing the "rescuing" —from fixing code or infrastructure at the system level, to monitoring dashboards and creating visibility into the systems at the operational level, to developing and refining the stats and reports that were needed to pinpoint issues. It was all hands-on deck, with new hands and those that were there prior to launch.

Sure, we needed the help, and it was a great thing for the program. But as I said earlier, it's not about the individual efforts, it's about the collective efforts and taking the good with the bad. The rescue story completely discounted the previous three years of work by thousands of people across the country and it seemed a bit too focused on who the "rescuers" were and how they individually brought success to a disastrous situation. And again, I will be the first to say thank you to anyone who showed up to help, whether you changed careers to work on the ACA back in 2010 or you showed up a month after rollout.

Another key fact that did not come out of the narrative has to do with asking the following question: Why didn't help arrive before the launch? This is a very logical question to ask because given the extreme challenges I outlined throughout the book, it was not a well-hidden secret that it was a high-risk proposition to scope, define, and deliver an MVP by a fixed launch date. Plus, my team of federal staff and contractors were stretched pretty thin supporting the vast range of requirements and stakeholders. In fact, I briefed Todd Park numerous times on the status of the project and pleaded for high-caliber IT professionals to come in to help in any way—specifically to improve the ability to launch—but for the life of me, I could not understand why that was not taken more seriously. After the launch, the mad scramble began to corral all the help we could get. Todd then managed to recruit the first wave of people to come in and start the so-called "rescue."

In today's world of rapid news cycles and fierce competition for eyeballs, facts are substituted with opinions. Regardless of truth and authenticity of information, as long as enough people believe something is true, then it must be true. The narrative of having HealthCare.gov rescued is attractive and effective in shifting the attention from what went wrong to what was being done. Everyone who worked to improve the situation watched this narrative unfold and rather than feeling demoralized, we all welcomed any help we could get. We embraced the attention that descended on the project post-launch and how it helped to accelerate efforts to shore up resources to solve the biggest problems. And without fanfare, we quietly proceeded to continue our job we all had committed to do years before the launch.

Another longer-term issue with the rescue narrative is the unabashed claiming to be a part of the so-called rescue. Shortly after HealthCare.gov began to stabilize, many of the people that came to CMS to help shift gears began to position themselves to do business with CMS for the long-term. They'd market themselves and conduct business development activities, spring boarding from the Health-Care.gov rescue activities. I began to see business cards and websites of companies set up by several of the former rescuers that used some form of the motto "we rescued HealthCare.gov." Starting in 2015, many of these companies have won lucrative contracts with CMS and the VA.

In some cases, it's representative of the culture of entitlement, where taking credit for an outcome has little to do with your actual contribution. Remember, the narrative paints this picture of personal sacrifice and motivation rooted in noble commitments to noble causes. The outcome created by the people that claim they were part of the rescue is quite different than what you might envision, where people make great personal sacrifices, and then after they perform their service, they return to what they did before. That's not the case. You have to be extremely naïve to think that when conquerors finish conquering, they then go back home. Conquerors always then become colonists, which in this case, translated to nesting comfortably in federal government contracts after two to three months of great personal sacrifice.

Mikey Dickerson, who is most well-known to be the lead on the "rescue," however, did not start a company to do business with the government. The story is, Todd Park convinced him to return in 2014 to serve as the Administrator of the US Digital Services. In early 2017, because Mikey's position was a political appointment, he had to exit with the administration. When Mikey departed government, he immediately became an advisor to Nava PBC, a tech company started by a couple of HealthCare.gov "rescuers" that now have government contracts with CMS. Mikey likely is constrained by government ethics policies that restricts unethical activities.[4] All the "rescuers" have done well in capitalizing on an opportunity, including Andy Slavitt, who is pictured in Brill's Time magazine article as part of the rescue. At that time, he was the Group Executive Vice President for Optum, a United Health Group subsidiary who in 2014 first became Principal Deputy Administrator at CMS and then went on to become the Acting Administrator of CMS.[5] No problem there, right? After all this is America at its finest—where everyone is created equally but opportunity is something you have to create for yourself.

In a FCW article published in May 2015, Mikey Dickerson was quoted on several observations he had on HealthCare.gov back in 2013. Mikey said the following:

---

4   "After Leaving Government," United States Office of Government Ethics, https://www.oge.gov/web/oge.nsf/Resources/After+Leaving+Government

5   Jon Reid, "Acting CMS Head Still Being Vetted," Morning Consult, August 27, 2015, https://morningconsult.com/2015/08/27/acting-cms-head-still-being-vetted-after-more-than-a-year-on-the-job/

"One was that there was no monitoring of the production system. For those of you that run large distributed systems, you will understand that this is as if you are driving a bus with the windshield covered," he said. "Second was that there were hundreds of people and dozens of companies involved, but nobody in charge. Third was that there was no particular urgency about the situation. As I would come to understand, nobody was acting like there was anything out of the ordinary because there was nothing out of the ordinary."

He wasn't happy with the status quo that produced the site either. "The whole system had worked as normal and produced the expected result, which was a website that was overpriced by hundreds of millions of dollars and did not work, at all," he said.

With the numerous basic problems, he told the White House he could fix it well enough to enroll four million people but would have to stay on to follow through. "My three-day trip had turned into a nearly three-month stint," he said.

Dickerson said his invoice for the nine-week period from October to Dec. 31 showed he worked an average of 17.5 hours per day. "I was hallucinating and having other problems from not having slept enough for three months. This was the hardest thing I have ever done and I hope nothing ever comes close to it again," he said.[6]

---

6   Mark Rockwell, "Mikey Dickerson on failures and fixes," FCW, March 27, 2015,
     https://fcw.com/articles/2015/03/27/dickerson-at-sxsw.aspx

Mikey's point one is absolutely correct. We had little to no automated, active monitoring of the system. We had begun to instrument specific choke points that were identified but as of October 18 when the first "rescue" crew was briefed and we immediately went to work on acquiring and implementing monitoring tools, the manual instrumentation effort was then overtaken by the use of tools.

Mikey's second point was also entirely valid and was something many agreed on including the OIG published case study on HealthCare.gov saying there were numerous missteps but, "Most critical was the absence of clear leadership …"[7]

Mikey's third point regarding observing there was a lack of urgency is an example of how a group of people can be in one room at the same time, hear and see the same things, and each person walks away with a completely different interpretations of what transpired, kind of like how eyewitness accounts are highly unreliable.[8]

I would venture to say that on behalf of everyone that was already on the team, other than the rescuers, we were calm, patient, receptive to input, willing to accept assistance, and ready to engage. Over the preceding three plus years, regardless of title and position, we had a fair amount of turnover for a range of reasons and anyone that was still present during launch weathered situations that drove quite a few people out. Staying and seeing it through was the goal and commitment of almost everyone. What good would it do to not be calm,

---

7   Daniel R. Levinson, "HeatlhCare.gov: Case Study of CMS Management of the Federal Marketplace," U.S. Department of Health and Human Services, Office of Inspector General, February 2016, https://oig.hhs.gov/oei/reports/oei-06-14-00350.pdf

8   Hal Arkowitz and Scott O. Lilienfeld, "Why Science Tells Us Not to Rely on Eyewitness Accounts," Scientific American, January 1, 2010, https://www.scientificamerican.com/article/do-the-eyes-have-it/

cool, and collected? I had met with several members of the rescue team after they met early in the morning of October 18, 2013 with our administrator, Marilyn Tavenner in DC. The van brought them over to the CMS offices in Baltimore and after a couple hours of providing the next level of detail and background, I arranged for them to meet some of the data services hub development team stationed in Columbia, MD. We agreed after they concluded in Columbia we would then regroup in CGI's office in Herndon, VA in the evening. This was where we kicked off the work together and rolled up our sleeves to first try to work on determining how to quickly obtain licenses for monitoring software such as New Relic. The operative words are "we" and "our," as we collectively moved with urgency, no different than we had moved up to October 18th. Mikey's gross mischaracterization made it sound like we were sitting around with no sense of just how bad things were. If the rescuers came in April, when I asked Todd Park to help obtain talent, I think on one hand, things would have been different because they would have seen what was going on before the launch, but on the other hand, if they experienced what we experienced prior to launch, they may have just given up and walked away from the chaos. In a way, because Mikey made this comment, it gives you a sense of his frame of mind at that time, which seems more like judging rather than listening, and thus, he misinterpreted calmness and patience in accepting newcomers into the fold as "lack of urgency."

Mikey said "As I would come to understand, nobody was acting like there was anything out of the ordinary because there was nothing out of the ordinary."[9] Another perspective is that the ordinary had

---

9   "Mikey Dickerson to SXSW: Why We Need You in Government," The U.S. Digital Service, Medium, 2015, https://medium.com/the-u-s-digital-service/mikey-dickerson-to-sxsw-why-we-need-you-in-government-f31dab3263a0

been total chaos and the teams were so beleaguered but still found the energy and passion to wake up each day and show up and be present to make lemonade out of lemons. I find it funny how, when Mikey was leaving his job as the Administrator of the US Digital Services, he posted final words of wisdom on Medium. In his post, he's said how difficult it had been and how "The team tends to poke fun at my flat affect and often serious facial expression …" Is it possible that others also can come across that way? Would anyone dare say that when things are difficult for Mikey, his expression says that nothing is out of the ordinary? Let's examine something else in his post. Mikey displayed the front and back of his Digital Services business card as part of this post and on both sides in different size letters there's the phrase "Don't Panic." The caption for the image of the card says, "My early (and still favorite) mantra." Maybe after almost four years of driving towards making the launch happen, we didn't spend a lot of time panicking. Maybe we were seasoned and weathered to take on this kind of chaotic work because we've seen and done similar things and made it through, on behalf of the people we serve. Maybe we were trying to be the voice and image of calm so others would not panic, especially the people we all worked for. Maybe after living through three years of toxic politics, including a government shutdown that overshadowed the launch, we had no choice but to be calm. And last but not least, maybe we lived a life where what we did and who we are was not printed on a business card.

In the article, Mikey goes on to say he was unhappy with the website that was overpriced by hundreds of millions of dollars and website that did not work at all. What was his basis of comparison? Could it be failed Google projects or investments? What was included on his tally that added up to "hundreds of millions" —

because The Washington Post had a real challenging time trying to track down what the figures actually were, including fact checking people such as the HHS Secretary, CGI, and David Powner from GAO, who sat next to me at a House hearing in November 2013.[10] There's a confusing relationship between how much the government initially budgets versus how much it is then apportioned by OMB to use, and how much is obligated to use versus how much and when figures are reported publicly versus how much it actually spent. This is a very elusive and confusing exercise to figure out the bottom line. And what I just outlined happens repeatedly though constant negotiation and passing back and forth from the different levels of government, each round reflecting adjustments made at the project level, program level, agency portfolio level, HHS department level, and at the OMB level. In addition, how wide you cast the net will yield you quite different answers. What's included in terms of contracts that support HealthCare.gov? According to the HHS/OIG, CMS had around sixty contracts for ACA and only six were consistently identified as IT contracts. If you only tallied up the six, you likely will be somewhere in the $350 million to $400 million according to my recollection, but very few people look deeper or don't know where to look, so they come up with erroneous numbers. If you were to just total up the Marketplace Call Center contract and the Eligibility Support Worker Contract, you would already be approaching $1 billion dollars. Even in all the hearings I was in or watched, these contracts were never counted in the costs—probably because no one

---

10   Glenn Kessler, "How much did HealthCare.gov cost?" Fact Checker, The Washington Post, October 24, 2013, https://www.washingtonpost.com/news/fact-checker/wp/2013/10/24/how-much-did-healthcare-gov-cost/?noredirect=on&utm_term=.3633698a68c8; Glenn Kessler, "How much did HealthCare.gov cost? (Part 2)," Fact Checker, The Washington Post, November 19, 2013, https://www.washingtonpost.com/news/fact-checker/wp/2013/11/19/how-much-did-healthcare-gov-cost-part-2/?utm_term=.f767a09fded0

asked. So where did Mikey get the numbers? It had to be a highly reliable source since he expressed a great level of conviction in saying it was overpriced.

Let's move on to the next set of assertions made by Mikey. He told the White House he could make the site work well enough to enroll 4 million people.[11] This number may be pretty close, given that he stayed on the project for less than four months. But by the end of the first year, there were approximately 6.8 million people covered by the Insurance Marketplaces, with about another 4.2 million people covered under the expanded Medicaid program in twenty-even states. I think Mikey either didn't know about Medicaid being part of the requirements or didn't realize there are different categories in various programs even though they started their application on HealthCare. gov. Next, he goes on to say a three-day trip turned in to nearly a three-month stint. I find it hard to be sympathetic, as some of us working on the Insurance Marketplace program clocked forty-five months as Mikey approached his third month.

Mikey states that his invoices showed that he worked an average of seventeen and a half hours a day from October to December 31st. Not trying to minimize the high number of hours, but since July 2013, some of my staff and myself were averaging eighteen to twenty hours a day. Big difference is, Mikey and the other "rescuers" were 1099s billing an average of two hundred dollars an hour for every hour worked—not a paltry sum for all that sacrifice.

The last paragraph from the FCW article is a real kicker. Mikey said he was "hallucinating and having other problems from not having slept enough for three months." Given the extreme sleep

---

11 "Mikey Dickerson to SXSW: Why We Need You in Government," The U.S. Digital Serivce, Medium, 2015, https://medium.com/the-u-s-digital-service/mikey-dickerson-to-sxsw-why-we-need-you-in-government-f31dab3263a0

deprivation from working endless hours for three months is certainly nothing to poke fun at, but I wonder if that makes all of us that ran the marathon from before March of 2010 to December 2013 some kind of robot because it certainly isn't human to push that hard for that long. I'm glad that Mikey had a good glimpse of what it's like in the long haul. Mikey also said, "This was the hardest thing I have ever done, and I hope nothing ever comes close to it again" and I believe the context includes the work on HealthCare.gov and his time as a federal executive running the US Digital Service, which puts Mikey somewhere between two to three years of service to the government, both as a 1099 and as a W2 employee. Again, I have to compare my twenty-one years and wonder: How the heck did I survive? Mikey certainly got it right by reflecting that it is really, really hard on you to be in public service, and I sense that this will have been the most memorable job he has to date. That is a badge he can wear, and the sense of pride deserves some recognition and respect. What if someone took over as the next Administrator of Digital Services and completely disregarded his two years of work, as if the beginning of time only commenced when the new person showed up? I venture to guess that the new person would come across as being quite narcissistic about their presence in the world.

It may seem like I am harboring some resentment for Mikey. You may think that I am not going to be able to thoroughly convince you that my purpose was to point to the actual events that happened with the same cast of people, but framed in a manner that just happens to be the truth—not my version of truth, but the simple truth: Todd, Mikey, and other rescuers are just people like you and me, and we all make mistakes, take things for granted, and in our passion and focus to execute and do some good, we forget to look up and see there are lots of people who are also there and are as involved as you. We all have a moral responsibility to truly represent the public's interest as career federal employees and contractors where, in our private lives, we would always want the people of our government to behave honorably, whether anyone is looking or not, and certainly not grandstand and think we are celebrity superheroes.

With all the hype around the good that the US Digital Services has done, I think something is missing and that might be the reality that not all things touched by any one group consistently results in success. I think it's healthy on occasion to exercise humility and reflect upon the successes and failures of your endeavors, to internally assess the good that you're capable of doing. Yet, at the same time, you should also recognize that not everything has worked out and that without factoring in failures, you won't truly have the experience to move forward. It puts who you were and who you are now in proper perspective, relative to what you have done. And maybe, it helps inform you of what you need to do and where to go next in your journey. Transforming or expanding access to health care is not a short-term endeavor, particularly when you are part of an imperfect system already working to implement another imperfect piece of legislation. It's about the long haul, a meaningful change that gets achieved across multiple generations.

I certainly do not want to come across as discouraging people from public service, but if you want to jump in, jump in with both feet and stay for more than just a couple of years to really gain perspective and a sense of ownership in a legacy you might want to leave behind, so that your children and grandchildren might not have to fight the same issues over again. Yes, certainly be part of something bigger than yourself, but do it for the full experience of all the good and bad that comes with driving change in the world. Don't be a tourist in public service and only look for the guaranteed, great experience without being a fully committed part of creating that experience.

NOT ALL COLLABORATIONS WORK OUT TO BE PRODUCTIVE AND GENUINE

From 2009 when I first met Todd when he joined the federal government as the HHS CTO, to just after the launch of HealthCare.gov—so, a span of about forty-five months—we closely collaborated on open data initiatives, the Medicare dashboard, the first HealthCare.gov launch in July, 2010, and numerous, excruciating all day ACA budget discussions to figure out how to implement 100 percent of all ACA requirements. This included all major non-Insurance Marketplace sections of ACA with only a fraction of the necessary budget. Working together on such a large canvas of critical initiatives was extremely invigorating, as Todd relied on my experience at CMS, insights, and frankness, and in return, I was energized by his sincerity, great ability to grasp the most complex matters, and drive to make a difference in the world. Todd would refer to me as his brother and it felt genuine, so in return, I began to really embrace him as a brother, an ally—someone that had the credibility and legitimacy to get people to pay attention to the realities and risks of what we were going through in the time leading up to the launch.

On several occasions in 2012 and 2013, I would assemble the key leads of the contractors and federal staff to brief Todd on progress being made—blockers preventing progress and raising significant risk, how to best work with dozens of number one priorities, and solicit Todd's assistance in brokering compromises between CMS, HHS, IRS, SSA, and OMB, and just being the broker of reason and rational decision-making so we could all have some clear path and direction forward.

In one of these twelve-plus hour briefings held in April of 2013, we were joined by several McKinsey consultants for discussion and to get a background for an assessment they were brought in to perform (was eventually called "Red Team Discussion Document").[12] I took the opportunity to ask Todd to advocate on behalf of my team to bring in four to six high-caliber technology people that not only understood technology, but how to work with the business teams to lead efforts to accelerate the process for prioritizing and defining requirements and translating them into building the MVP.

Somehow, even after dedicating a dozen hours going over all the issues and making a plea to bring in outside assistance, the request went unfulfilled. It would take until October 17th for that help to arrive, and from then on, as weeks went by, Todd began to distance himself from me and probably quite a few others in CMS, to the point where he no longer answered my calls, text, and emails. To this day, I have no confirmed explanation as to why our relationship became non-existent, but I suppose I can speculate that he may have been told to distance himself because of his proximity to the President. Whatever the reason may be, I am a bit saddened that we can't take a nice long drive and pick up a sack of Krystal burgers, like we did when we met with Oak Ridge National Laboratory on a project and Todd needed a ride back to the Knoxville airport from there. I wish we could look back and share the great stories of our experience working on ACA and have a long, healthy laugh about it all.

---

12   "McKinsey report on problems with HealthCare.gov," The Washington Post, https://www.washingtonpost.com/apps/g/page/politics/mckinsey-report-on-problems-with-healthcaregov/601/

CHAPTER 9

"MAINTAIN YOUR COLLABORATIVE SPIRIT"

A close personal friend of mine is a bit like me in terms of how we work—she's very passionate and motivated to solve problems. In some situations, that can be perceived by others as being overly aggressive, impatient, and not staying in your own "swim lane." And when someone on the receiving end of that passion is pushed too hard, or misperceives the intent, they're more likely to focus on the messenger rather than the message. Often an organization that prefers that people get along over getting work done, and believe producing results has little to no tolerance for people who make other people uncomfortable because they actually bring a novel idea to the table, can execute that idea faster and better than others.

So, rather than getting on the side of doing something right and better, my friend's supervisor advised her to "Maintain your collaborative spirit." That's code for "Let's keep ourselves in check and only introduce ideas when we know that people are ready to hear them." Kind of reminiscent of an old wine commercial where Orson Wells says, "We will sell no wine before its time." The trick is to know the best time to advocate for a better way to do things before opportunity slips away but not at the expense of someone else's hurt feelings.

That's relevant when working in an IT collaboration, where many stakeholders are guarding their perspectives and priorities, and your job, at least in theory, is to integrate all their requirements along a timeline that meets every stakeholder's needs. This can be a painful and protracted extraction and orchestration process, with a tremendous overhead in time spent on not just collaborating but also give-and-take negotiating. It can wear on you, but you have to maintain that collaborative spirit and gently drive people in the same direction.

AVOID THE "US-THEM"

In very tough situations such as working with the deadlines for the Insurance Marketplace program, it can be very difficult to keep a collaborative spirit. This happens because there's often a sense of "us-them." When a dozen policy teams are converging and trying to put all the requirements together, the last thing any of them wants is to feel like they have to get in line and somehow be subordinate to any other situation or priority. This is the self-centric nature of many individually responsible stakeholders that needs to be managed by a single individual empowered to arbitrate, mediate, and establish the path that all teams follow in order to get to the MVP for day one and beyond.

Unfortunately, often there are people who will find any way to get back on top if they and their requirements have been de-prioritized. And because HealthCare.gov lacked the designated single individual who would make calls, there was more than just a "backdoor" to get your say as to what was part of the MVP. In fact, there were so many ways to overrule and override—sometimes at the extreme expense of risking everything just to get their requirement included—that the definition of MVP eroded more and more due to the constant piling up on what was expected for day one.

A perfect example of this was an organization representing a block of issuers, insisting on adding logos to its products that would be displayed as part of a range of QHPs once HealthCare.gov processed enough information on the application to know the proper range of choices to display in what's called "plan compare." The plan compare feature shows those plans available in the applicant's service area that match or closely match their circumstance and any user defined filters. With significant delays all around—including the window for issuers to submit the

> **BECAUSE HEALTHCARE.GOV LACKED THE DESIGNATED SINGLE INDIVIDUAL WHO WOULD MAKE THE CALLS, THERE WAS MORE THAN JUST A "BACKDOOR" TO GET YOUR SAY AS TO WHAT WAS PART OF THE MVP.**

QHP products electronically for both CMS and the state insurance commissioners to review, which had already been significantly delayed from the logical window of time before the 2012 elections until April 2013—there was a rush to design the templates to be used for submitting the structured data that describes the QHP product. These included data such as maximum out-of-pocket limits, co-pays, deductibles, and coinsurance. There were over one thousand products across the thirty-six states that HealthCare.gov had to handle the data for.

Once the templates were finalized and the month of April 2013 window for submission opened and closed, the process for review and approval included a complex data exchange between the system CMS used for processing the submitted QHP data with the system used by the National Association of Insurance Commissioners (NAIC). This was done because approximately twenty-five states are mandated at the state government level to use NAIC's system for review and processing of the data submitted by issuers whereas the balance of the states use CMS' system. After exchange of data is complete, CMS is then able to have a complete aggregate of the issuer products for the thirty-six states in which HealthCare.gov requires in order to display the correct plan choices and all the associated data necessary to process the enrollments. The optimal and lowest-risk time to have thought about and included the logos to be displayed was during the QHP data submission process in April. Each company/product logo would accompany the electronic submission and be embedded as part of the set of structured data that ultimately is the source data for HealthCare.gov's plan compare feature. But that window of opportunity was missed and now it was June. Still, the organization came to CMS and insisted on submitting the logos late after the processing had already begun.

To accommodate the submission of the logos at this later date, and through a separate process to receive the data, process, and store the data—which, since it's outside the schedule that already had been executed—anything processed separately to link the logos to the originally submitted QHP data would (a) introduce yet another unplanned requirement that's outside the MVP, and (b) increase the probability of errors given the logos would be submitted separate, outside the normal process. I'm sure that some of you out there are saying, "No sweat, it would be so easy to do." And I would agree with you, if you would also consider that we were already so far behind that any rational person who could see the whole picture would surely deprioritize this added feature until we were able to safely roll out the initial production build.

I pushed back hard and said this little sidebar exercise would take away from an already overburdened team that is dealing with delivering the MVP and would jeopardize an already risky situation even more. You would think that reason would prevail and everyone would at least respect the possibility that it would be an unnecessary risk to take amid all that was happening. I absolutely get it that these organizations have decades of investments in building their brand awareness, and that much of it rides on their logo. But it was time to shed more of those requirements that had only recently begun to gel to keep the focus on some version of an MVP, and it certainly was not a time to load up more requirements.

After I said no the first time, the situation kept coming up, over and over again. The first request came through various staff in the teams that managed the QHP function and the plan compare feature. I explained the high-risk situation and provided the reasoning behind why I said no. Then came direct phone calls to me, in which I repeatedly explained why I said no. The next attempt was by way of the CMS administrator and chief of staff, who both genuinely believed my explanation but as a courtesy to the industry association, brought me back to the table to ask if this was feasible in terms of not taking away or risking what was already slated to be on the MVP path. Again, I politely pushed back and said no, and to their credit, they supported not taking the unnecessary risk. From there it went to the HHS, and next to White House personnel, and each time I again explained why. Luckily, either we just ran out of time to kick the idea around as the summer of 2013 started and everything that was delayed was converging, or the industry organization finally wore down and accepted that no meant no. I tried to be extremely collaborative in working with the industry overall by facilitating the development of features that integrate the new HealthCare.gov mode of shopping online for health insurance with their existing abilities and their way of conducting business with new customers.

Maintaining a collaborative spirit is certainly part of the approach to working with multiple stakeholders, but at the same time you can't possibly cater to everyone's needs 100 percent of the time.

Maintaining a collaborative spirit isn't something that individuals do only to get along in a crowd trying reach an agreement on something. And maintaining a collaborative spirit only means something if people are doing it for something bigger than themselves. If they don't do that, then things actually start falling apart.

CHAPTER 10

HOW MUCH CHANGE IS REALISTIC?

The ACA Insurance Marketplaces were created to provide access to affordable health-care coverage through an online application process with real-time results of the application, process requests for financial assistance, and the enrollment process completed within a significantly shorter time compared to the pre-ACA ways of applying for coverage. The final result represented some of the most significant changes in how Insurance companies operate, with "affordable" coverage including coordination with a state's Medicaid and CHIP program to enroll members of a household in the appropriate health-care plan whether government sponsored or through the QHP products available through various issuers.

But what happened behind the scenes to ensure that every person who enrolled was guaranteed coverage meant major changes in the industry. Without even considering the effort to translate the policies into requirements and business rules, there had to be significant changes in how business was conducted between issuers that offered health plan products and insurance regulators at the state level, the federal government, and involved agencies in facilitating offsets to premiums through an APTC, and numerous other changes that were part of the insurance reform provisions in other parts of the ACA.

If you were to trace all the changes that had to happen before the launch of HealthCare.gov—and even after the plan year changes every January 1—you would be amazed at how much was done, not in perfect unison, but all adhering to the same timeline. Looking at the overall impact of the new program on the entire US health-care landscape, you can also see where improvements can be made and how much progress has been truly made in the effort to reduce the number of uninsured in the United States. There are approximately twenty million more people able to access health care today than only a few years ago, where many people were constantly living in fear that they wouldn't be able to afford decent health care. But is that the finish line? While twenty million more people having access to affordable health care is certainly a major accomplishment, isn't it just the first major increment toward the goal of everyone having health insurance coverage?

With projects the near the magnitude of the ACA Insurance Marketplaces, framing the reality of how much change can be achieved relative to how much change is expected and how much is realistic in a given time frame is key, but to properly frame the conversation and truly work on behalf of the people, you have to be open and transparent about the effects of the policies, whether they are intended, unintended, or unknown.

In the political arena, where much of this plays out, it's more about political gamesmanship than the substance of the policies, which would otherwise have a better chance of positively transforming some aspect of the health-care system rather than getting mired in extreme views and rhetoric that distorts and derails any effort to be open and honest. In this era of highly toxic politics and playing to the populist movement, genuine efforts to reform anything, including health care, will be questionable as to the authenticity in improving the status quo.

But let's leave the political observations for a bit and take an optimistic view of the intended changes of the ACA. First there are sections of the law directed toward health insurance reform, such as medical loss ratio (MLR) and rate review (RR) to keep insurance companies' profits in check and to make sure profit margins above a certain threshold are factored back in to the benefits equation for the policyholders. Then there are sections that attempt to provide for greater consumer protections and greater transparency of information provided by the insurance companies to aid consumers in making decisions on their coverage and in understanding the cost of their coverage and care, although the present administration has given the green light to sell products that do not comply with consumer protections under the ACA.

Another is setting a new standard, a benchmark for insurance companies to provide products that meet a minimum set of essential health benefits (EHB) so that consumers are better able to compare costs across health plan products, since all have to meet the minimum standards, but the present administration and Congress continue to try to weaken these consumer protection-driven aspects of the ACA. Then, of course there's the establishment of Insurance Marketplaces in conjunction with the option to expand Medicaid within each state. These include the requirement for state insurance commissioners and the CCIIO oversight group in CMS to jointly review, approve, and coordinate the QHP data that would be the key health plan product information needed by consumers to make an appropriate selection that meets their coverage and cost needs, including the amount of APTC if they qualify and elected to receive the premium assistance. These are just portions of what ACA changed across the vast and complex health-care landscape. ACA also demanded a tremendous amount of change for federal agencies and insurance companies, a huge business transformation challenge. It was much more in-depth than simply building technology; first and foremost, ACA was about changing how organizations and people conducted their business in providing and purchasing health insurance products, which involved extensive business process reengineering efforts—much tougher to do than just building the supporting technology.

Aside from HealthCare.gov as a supersize example, there are other great examples, such as the menu of services you can get online at SSA.gov and the IRS providing the Free File software to file your tax return on its site. It took many years, cautious risk assessments, and a few incidents along the way for government to move from every service being an in-person session—because that was the only way to "authenticate" you—to now having an equal level of confidence that a person interacting via the internet is actually who they say they are.

Across all the government programs, the need for change was recognized a long time ago, but no agency recklessly races out and sets up online services until internal policies, processes, capabilities, support arrangements, and the level of responsiveness and meaningful interaction between systems of record and a consumer interface can be placed in an online engagement scenario. We appear to be in the middle of a trend towards overemphasizing agile approaches and user experience above the importance of first understanding requirements and how to integrate what is coming out of the agile process and front-end user experience with operations and back end data.

The overemphasis on agile and user experience comes from the infiltration of the idea that whatever is used in modern tech approaches in the private, for-profit business model transfers to 100 percent of what government enterprises are trying to achieve. Much of it can and does help with accelerating progress made in implementation of technologies required for public programs, but there's also less regard for the much harder parts, which are security, protecting data, integration with other systems and data sources, just to name a few. With all things being equal in terms of resources, constraints, and the products to be delivered to market, the government can move at the same velocity as any other sector, but in the end it would not sacrifice security and privacy protection requirements.

I hope my explanation and examples regarding how much change can be expected for transforming the health-care programs and the underlying technology provides for a better understanding of the forces in play so that you can see how it isn't possible for government to innovate at an accelerated pace. With greater understanding of the underlying motivators and constraints placed on government relative to the expectations for rapid change, perhaps we can have more meaningful debates and critiques about, for example, how to improve the health-care system. And as for government being able to rapidly adapt to and embrace change as if it were a small start-up, I think in the end we would want our government to err on the side of caution in embracing new technologies and implementing these technologies in a secure and supported manner.

MY "WORLD-CLASS EXPERIENCE"

Every time I think back to the discussion on how we needed to produce a world-class experience for consumers of HealthCare.gov, I compare situations that I have personally experienced as a consumer in working with online powerhouses like Amazon. As I mentioned before, it really isn't an apples-to-apples comparison, but let's do a comparison so that you can see how consumer transactions online have perfected the consumer experience.

I ordered three items from Amazon—a couple of power cables and an entry-level drone (just for fun). According to the order tracking, all three items were shipped under one UPS tracking number. When the package arrived, I opened it and the contents were two glass water bottles, which I had not ordered. I then logged into my Amazon account, which had noted that all three items I had ordered were delivered under the correct tracking number. So it wasn't like I received the wrong package. I received a box that was labeled correctly and tracked correctly, but the contents were incorrect. It took a while to click through all the customer assistance links, and after fifteen minutes of poking around I found the feature to enter information about the issue using a series of templates that were developed for every problem—except for the one I had. So I filled out the forms to best reflect the situation. But because of the template, it appeared that I wanted to return my merchandise, not that I wanted to return the water bottles and still have my original order shipped to me. I finally made it through the feature, and at the end of the process I selected the option for Amazon to call me right away.

Within ten seconds, the phone rang. It was a customer service representative in the Philippines. The caller ID number came up as Seattle, I suppose given Amazon's offices there. So the call was routed to the company's call centers around the world and it wound up in the Philippines. But the conversation with the rep just went around and around as follows:

I informed the rep that I had ordered three items and had received notification that they were shipped under one UPS tracking number, and that when the package arrived, the contents were not what I ordered. The tracking number outside the box, I explained, matched the notification that I received about the three items that I ordered being shipped under a single tracking number.

"Just return the merchandise," I was told.

"Well, how do I get the right merchandise?" I asked.

"Let me understand. You received the box. It's the right tracking number. You opened the box. But it's not what you ordered?" the help desk person said.

"Yes, but how do I get the right merchandise?" I asked.

"Just return the merchandise."

After about twenty minutes of the same circular conversation, I asked for the supervisor, who informed me that there was no way she could order the merchandise for me. "The best I can do is give you credit on Amazon Prime, like a shopping card," she said. "And the two glass water bottles? Ah, just forget it. Keep them."

After nearly an hour of wrestling with this at two o'clock in the morning, I started thinking, "Yeah, this is my Amazon world-class experience."

If this "world-class experience" is an example of what to expect, what does that say about optimizing the user experience in health care?

The Amazon model isn't so much about people. It's about people's money, their purchasing power. When you talk about change in health care versus change in e-commerce, the motivating factors are drastically different. Because what is a good thing in public policy doesn't translate into the same thing on the private side, and there are good reasons why. The Amazon call center, for instance, is designed to help the company be competitive in the business world. But federal government programs are barred from using offshore resources, so if you call 1-800-MEDICARE, you'll never be routed out of the United States. That's intended to help people feel secure and safe about their information.

What is the definition of change? In the case of the US health-care system, can it really change to the extent that it looks like e-commerce? Sure, there are good and bad things that could be selectively chosen. But overall, a blanket statement such as "world-class experience" doesn't equate to the same thing. How would doctors and hospitals respond if we declared we expected a "world-class experience?" Would they know exactly how to create that experience for us? Would it be meals ordered from Michelin star restaurants and not a food service contractor making ten thousand meals a day, memory foam slippers instead of the socks with the tacky material, and Egyptian cotton gowns that don't require eight arms to tie the strings in the back?

MIND THE FRAME OF REFERENCE

When working on projects requiring so much change, one of the first factors to consider is: How much change is realistic? That starts by figuring out the definition of "change." Who is defining it, and by what version of reality? What's your frame of reference in determining the magnitude of change, and what is realistic in a given situation? In the case of the Insurance Marketplace program, there had to be a fair sense of how the current individual market worked or didn't work, how Medicaid worked with or without ACA expansion rules, the current capabilities of the eight federal programs that needed to provide data in real time, and thousands of other "current states" and paths to "future state" situations. If you don't know where you start your journey, then how do you know how far you have to go?

Often the ability or will to lead or drive change is time constrained, especially if you hold an elected position. Earlier in the book, I spoke of the motivating factors driven by the cycles of elections, and how much change can be achieved may be a function of how much time is on the clock. Remember that political realities are often term driven, and you can't drive change if you're not in office, so you devote a lot of time, energy, and resources to getting reelected, which then makes you a professional politician. Professional politicians often are motivated to lead or drive change based on what pollsters say and whether the effort to drive change adds to their win factor or somehow upsets their party leadership and voter base. The reality for defining, leading, driving, and pursuing change may not be about the greater good for the public or nation, but rather a greater good for a much narrower range of constituencies.

What that boils down to is what the frame of reference is for determining what success looks like if your election cycles are two, four, six, or some other number of years. The shorter the cycle, the more you have to target key fund-raising candidates to beef up your war chest. The longer the cycle, the less you might have to move at a frenzied pace in focusing your energies on fund-raising and reelection. And all of that political professionalism distorts how much change is desired, by what deadline, and at what cost—with all three of those factors not necessarily adequately coordinated. Those factors form at least some outposts on what's operating between those boundaries. If politics are involved or if, in the corporate world, factors like tenure are involved, then those will play into the constraints of what frames true change.

As I mentioned earlier, a lot of ACA and its administrative processes are seen as burdensome to doctors. My primary care physician is part of a practice that's very successful. But at the end of the day, he's successful not entirely because he's rated by how many patients he's saved. He's also successful because he is still in business and practicing medicine. But he has to work with the insurance companies. He has to have a very good office manager. He has to have a billing service to optimize his revenue cycles, get paid, and meet his payroll. He has to do all those things in addition to practicing medicine. So when debating about health care or the quality of care, what's really happening in these provider settings? Debating about the fact that health care needs to be changed is one thing, but debating about how to do it is something else entirely, because it often doesn't take into account what's happening in the provider setting or all the people affected at the point of care.

So how do politicians with their underlying motivators to survive as a politician—the weight of constituencies, polling results, deals on and under the table, deals outside over dinner and drinks, fund-raising, and so forth—come up with legislation that actually recognizes the realities of what my primary care doctor faces on a daily basis? Politicians need to take a course on user experience design for the people who have to implement their legislation and the people who have to live and operate within the confines of their legislation.

RELATIVE TECHNOLOGY CHANGES

It isn't so much that technology is forever changing. It's always relative to the starting point of an organization that is thinking about a path forward. Often, when an organization is implementing a new program, it may need to develop a solution using a different approach and/or different technologies than what it has already spent years investing in. But what typically happens in most organizations is that things rarely start anew, as if working from a clean sheet of paper and only looking at the new without being encumbered and worrying about the old.

In reality, there are legacy software, systems, data, and processes to contend with. There may not even be an issue with legacy, but all that exists across the landscape of enterprise systems must still be contended with. When trying to interface to an existing system that processes and stores needed systems of record data, that's when you discover all the shortsighted, short-term solutions that were implemented with no effort to go back and apply a long-term solution.

Encountering all the legacy issues, including all the bad decisions that were made in the past due to lack of funding, time, resources, and so on, is what the Software Engineering Institute refers to as accumulated technical debt. This is a bit like when I was foolish enough to take on a kitchen and eat-in area remodeling project, where one of the first steps was to remove the 1960s wood paneling before applying a primer coat and then a fresh coat of paint. But underneath the paneling I discovered not one, but two layers of wallpaper, and after days of painfully scraping those away, I found an uneven coat of joint compound that had to be sanded down before I could even begin applying a coat of primer. That was my journey of discovering the house's "technical debt," and all of that had to be addressed in order to have a clean start. Building new systems and integrating with existing systems is magnitudes more difficult.

Any organization working under tight deadlines will accrue some level of technical debt, because prior projects and initiatives without time and resources but on tight deadlines will resort to short-term solutions, or what is commonly referred to as "temporary" solutions—as if there will ever be a conscious effort to go back to a longer-lasting solution. The passage of time and new priorities and urgencies prevent even an overt willingness to transform the temporary into a permanent solution. Thus, temporary becomes the permanent, and that trade-off will not reveal itself until the next project comes along and encounters the less-than-optimal circumstance. At that point, project members will have to decide to fix the sins of the past or also accept the less-than-optimal situation and continue forward until some new event or requirement forces the organization to confront the reality that whatever was temporary in the past is no longer sustainable going forward.

It's rather naïve in taking on a new project to think that contemporary approaches such as user experience design, agile development practices, cloud computing, open source software, APIs, and Everything-as-a-Service are immediate and guaranteed recipes for success. You still need implementable requirements—enough of them to start with an initial MVP. You must also understand the integration challenges between existing and new, the interfaces, data flows, systems of record/provenance of the data, the complex business rules applied to the data that may need to be ingested in the new system, the temporal effects and volatility of the data, the allowable uses and disclosure policies applied to the data, the boundaries and methods that were used to secure the data, and the types of encryption, hashing, or compression applied to the data.

Certainly, all the contemporary approaches have a great potential for accelerating and raising the probability of success in a software development project, but that presumes the organization sponsoring and/or owning the project is able to guide the build and delivery of products in workable units while adding more features as more is known about the project. What if the project is guided by a massive, complex piece of legislation in which decision making and decision makers of the policies and requirements go through a lengthy vetting process just to arrive at a high-level conceptual, notional view of what the product(s) need to be, and then that view is dispersed to dozens if not hundreds of stakeholders to render the next levels of detail to implement in their respective environments? In the effort to stand up HealthCare.gov, I think it's safe to say that all the teams did whatever they could to take increments of known requirements and build as much as they knew based on best available information. No one can claim it was a purist interpretation of agile, waterfall, or any other approach. And perhaps it's best to just refer to it as "hybrid" and whatever it took to get the job done. That is the real frame of reference, and not a theoretical discussion and lesson about the relative merits of agile versus waterfall. It's more about recognizing what it takes to get something done, and if that means taking the best parts of every approach that ever existed, including coming up with an ad hoc, new approach to get the job done, well, that then becomes the "appropriate" approach for the circumstance.

RATE OF CHANGE WITH ENTRENCHED SYSTEMS

Technology innovation can only move at a certain rate of change, and when an organization becomes so entrenched in so many other trade-offs made in the existing systems, it's difficult to escape the old when trying something new. The tendency then is to build something very similar to what already exists. And that applies to many areas of operations, not just technology. The question then becomes: How much change can realistically be expected? How much change can you tolerate in a short time if you're carrying all of your previous investments and trade-offs?

On July 30, 1965, President Lyndon B. Johnson signed into law the Social Security Act Amendments of 1965, which enacted the Medicare and Medicaid programs. In 2015, Medicare and Medicaid celebrated their fiftieth birthdays, and during a half century of congressional sessions, seven presidencies, and countless state legislative sessions and governorships, the two programs weathered many changes of varying magnitudes, and now collectively serve over 120 million people. To date, no one would say the programs have been perfected—after fifty-plus years, there are still struggles to accommodate challenges brought on by legislative policy changes, growth in participation on the beneficiary side and the health-care provider side, scale of operations, growing complexity in how payments are calculated and made, and consolidations from both the industry side and internally with respect to operations. There isn't really a point where these programs are put in place and someone calls them "done." It is an endless proposition to implement public policy that is intended to last several lifetimes. So the size of the measuring stick can tell different stories depending on whether you look at one legislatively driven change or many over the course of a decade.

There have been numerous analyses performed on the efficacy of policies in producing better health outcomes. Yet to this day, CMS is still in the process of implementing the latest round of major changes brought on by the Medicare Access and CHIP Reauthorization Act (MACRA), which was passed in 2015. CMS is also working on further stabilization and improvements to the Insurance Marketplace program created under the ACA in 2010 and building the new Quality Payment Program, spring boarding from the previously established provisions under the Health Information Technology for Economic and Clinical Health (HITECH) Act, which was passed in 2009. This continuous wave after wave of change doesn't even account for the natural changes that occur without a single new piece of legislation. There are cost-of-living increases to factor into the Part B premium in Medicare, payments to providers adjustments, aging technology that needs to be refreshed or modernized, and numerous other regulatory and mandatory activities the agency and programs have to perform on a cyclical basis. And through all of these changes and more, it's possible to connect the dots of what was done and see how fast and dangerous each new project descends with its own deadlines.

So, how much change can realistically be done in a few short years, or one generation or multiple generations, when the change you are implementing is layered on top of nearly every other change that is already in play? What short-term trade-offs must be made to incrementally sustain something beyond even what it was expected to last?

A key body in the federal government that on limited occasions asks this question is the OMB. The OMB controls the elements of the president's budget used across various agencies and programs, but when the layers of wall covering are peeled back revealing yet more wall covering, the tendency is to not take on the root issue and just move on funding the new as if it were mutually exclusive with what is already in place. It is this nonsensical budget process that spends half the time looking across the horizon and the remainder of the time burying its head in the sand that also contributes to the schizophrenic-like actions of the federal government. Guess what flows from that budget process? Yes, it's the contracting and hiring processes.

What are the prospects of having a consumer-facing program and its systems operate in an integrated fashion on behalf of the consumer if everything before the technology, policies, budgeting, contracts, and HR processes is not "integrated" in terms of a strategy and thought process? When that happens, the top-line budget becomes individual streams of funding, ever more splintered as it flows into the departments, agencies, programs, business components, and tech components, where each reports their artificial representations of "portfolios" so that OMB can track at the macro level, which has to do more with understanding how much you are spending than balancing it with how you are spending and who else in the government is actually doing something very similar. These are the institutionalized components of the massive machinery that tried to operate year to year under continuing resolutions rather than stable budgets. Some of the results seen with HealthCare.gov were also rooted in what I described above—I saw those scenarios unfold in the first four years after the ACA was signed into law.

The Insurance Marketplace program/HealthCare.gov launched at about 12:20 a.m. on October 1, 2013, and there was still more work to do in terms of functionality, efficiencies, automation, and improvements to processing data across multiple agencies and with insurance companies. And that will continue with each change that CMS takes on—which, in my twenty-one years, remained constant. CMS is the engine room of US health care that Congress and the presidency use to affect the rest of the health care and health insurance universe; attempts to disrupt health care in the United States, starting with CMS, will likely continue. That is the place to be if you want to be in the middle of any storm of disruption to health care. CMS needs people who are committed and dedicated for the long term and has less use for people who only want to be a health-care transformation "tourist."

CHAPTER 11

PUBLIC/PRIVATE SECTORS WORKING TOGETHER

Why can't the government operate more like the private sector? That's a question I've heard often throughout my career. I've already stated that the two have different sets of motivational factors. In most corporations, everything is about profit, and much of the motiva tion for making change and achieving some transformation is about improving the bottom line. Most corporations are for-profit organizations, and therefore everything is evaluated and executed based on that prevailing mindset. On the other hand, most government or pseudo-government-like agencies and programs are for people and not for profit. That starting frame of reference creates an entirely different path for each type of organization in making choices about how to execute change and what change can actually be undertaken.

There are numerous situations where the private sector would not, on its own, risk stepping in to raise the level of substandard access to housing, health care, utilities, transportation, and social services. Key decision points for the private sector are based on the assessment of risk versus return, return on investment, opportunity cost, and other factors. In these situations, when government works in conjunction with the private sector, it is possible for great things to happen. But the government, through its regulatory and enforcement powers, can create inducements or incentives to make it less risky and more attractive for the private sector to participate.

The Insurance Marketplaces provide APTCs for applicants who qualify based on their level of income in comparison to what is defined as the federal poverty level (FPL), and there is a second, smaller inducement called the cost-sharing reductions (CSR); both are paid to the insurance company. This makes it more attractive for insurance companies to operate in service areas they may not choose to cover without the inducements. It's a win-win situation, because people who need and ask for financial assistance receive offsets to their premium and cost share of the benefits they use, and the insurance companies are guaranteed to receive these payments to help offset their risk in offering coverage in certain areas. This may not ever be discussed under the public-private partnership umbrella, because the topic of ACA, HealthCare.gov, and Insurance Marketplaces are all ascribed as Obamacare—which demonizes the whole topic. So the partnerships and inducements to the insurance companies are hardly ever discussed in a positive manner or with an accompanying dose of economic realism about government creating artificially induced market forces to get the right people and organizations to play.

It's the same approach used thousands of times throughout history. Just take a look at our tax code, farm subsidies, energy subsidies, and government-backed insurance pools for flood, natural disaster, bank and industry bailouts, and mortgages. Often legislation is created first and foremost for the public good, but by the time it's signed into law and implemented, so much private sector input has woven its incentives and inducements in via whatever channel of influence.

So, when looking at the amount of change that's actually doable, begin by asking a couple of key questions: What are you changing? Is the industry public or private? Then, you must have adequate information to determine how the public and private sectors work together: What should they work on that shares similar motivations? What should they avoid because they have very different and contradictory motivations?

As I mentioned earlier in the book, the way the federal government traditionally communicates with the general "public"—commercial companies, individuals, trade associations, third parties representing constituencies, and even other government bodies such as state and local governments—is through the rule-making process. The rule-making process allows the public to comment on an initial version of the regulation, and then the comments received from the public are categorized and used in the preamble of the final regulation to indicate that major concerns have been acknowledged and/ or addressed in shaping the final regulation. Often, the archaic way in which the government goes through its policy development and sharing for public comment is very parochial, because there is a desire to avoid creating an uneven playing field by interacting with various outside groups and not using the rule-making process to communicate and receive feedback. In reality, throughout the process, specific interest groups that want their perspective accounted for in the regulation will go through any means to apply some pressure on the agencies that own the regulation. This is another example of how there's some level of communication and limited interaction between various groups that are part of the larger "public" and the government agencies that are responsible for implementing and overseeing the operation of their respective programs.

In truth, there is an inherent reality in how much the government can actually be committed in terms of a public-private partnership without creating an uneven playing field. A lot of things that the government does create opportunities for the private sector, either when contracting with the federal government or when being more competitive because of certain information that they have. And it's illegal to share policy information that is being developed, which can lead to fines and even jail time. Career staff are often reminded of this—through training, coaching, mentoring, and by the watchful eyes of dedicated procurement staff trying to ensure there are no unfair advantages. Political appointees, the staff they bring in, and others who are politically affiliated also receive training, but often walk on or very close to the boundaries to ensure the agenda handed to them is executed.

Still, what's needed is a much more collaborative model. Public-private partnerships do happen today. But sometimes they are only about changing perception and not reality. And they happen very situationally—often because they are based on the amount of risk an agency is willing to take to engage the outside world without giving anything away.

So risk goes hand-in-hand with public-private partnerships. But the framework for evaluating and taking on risk is different for for-profit organizations versus for-people organizations.

THE OIG REPORT

Earlier, I mentioned a report issued by the OIG that looked back at the HealthCare.gov rollout.

The report, titled "CMS Management of the Federal Marketplace," was largely written from source material, including all of the emails that I had generated from as far back as the report auditors required. Thousands of my emails were read and forwarded on to Congress, the OIG, and the Government Accountability Office (GAO). My emails were pretty popular back then with congressional committees, staffers, journalists, and anyone with a WordPress account and an opinion to share about what exactly they thought went wrong. You can imagine how some of the more colorful ways that I conveyed urgency to elicit a reaction made for great source material to selectively extract my statements. The OIG, in its due-diligence efforts to link all the key events and to provide as much of an objective narrative as possible, did a rather good job in pointing to the sources of the issues. I was told that, for the case study and for many other audits that were conducted on the Insurance Marketplace program, my emails were a good source of information, because while I was colorful, I also did not mince words. It was good to have some affirmation that at least I was consistent in my attempt to get people's attention.

The OIG report is one of the more accurate accounts of the ACA implementation, from passage of the law to the initial rollout. But as with any audit report, whether in the public or private sector, it basically attempted to conduct forensics. That's a little bit like trying to take the hamburger and reconstitute the cow. You can get to the shape of a cow, but it's not really a cow.

One of the key findings of the audit that the report is based on was that there was no single entity in charge of the delivery of HealthCare.gov, which is true. I was frustrated by the lack of recognition of how dangerous it was for everyone to keep spewing their demands and to keep politically manipulating and maneuvering without recognizing the consequences, and frustrated that the consequences would be something I would have to face and explain, which is why earlier in the book I mentioned that you have to own it. Embracing and acknowledging the fact that you step into the fray and are willing to speak for the problems is better than someone else trying to tag you.

FROM THE EXECUTIVE SUMMARY OF "HEALTHCARE. GOV: CMS MANAGEMENT OF THE FEDERAL MARKET-PLACE—A CASE STUDY"

The development of HealthCare.gov faced a high risk of failure, given the technical complexity required, the fixed deadline, and a high degree of uncertainty about mission, scope, and funding. Still, we found that HHS and CMS made many missteps throughout development and implementation that led to the poor launch. Most critical was the absence of clear leadership, which caused delays in decision making [sic], lack of clarity in project tasks, and the inability of CMS to recognize the magnitude of problems as the project deteriorated. Additional HHS and CMS missteps included devoting too much time to developing policy, which left too little time for developing the website; making poor technical decisions; and failing to properly manage its key website development contract. CMS's organizational structure and culture also hampered progress, including poor coordination between policy and technical work, resistance to communicating and heeding warnings of "bad news," and reluctance to alter plans in the face of problems. CMS continued on a failing path to developing HealthCare.gov despite signs of trouble, making rushed corrections shortly before the launch that proved insufficient. These structural, cultural, and tactical deficiencies were particularly problematic for HealthCare.gov given the significant challenges of implementing a new program involving multiple stakeholders and a large technology build.

Source: "HealthCare.gov: CMS Management of the Federal Marketplace—A Case Study," US Department of Health and Human Services, Office of the Inspector General, February 2016. OEI-06-14-00350.

At one point, I finally asked the chief operating officer of CMS to put me in charge. I knew that would not go over well; how could a technical person possibly understand what needed to be delivered on the program side?

Still, I was at the point of wanting to do just that. Ever since I first held a title of "chief something," I had focused on the big picture of the projects I was involved in. When you're thinking about the big picture, you're considering the convergence of everything that it takes to deliver contracts, budgets, people, technology, policy, processes, and partners. If your goal in life is to only command a small piece of that, and everything else is somebody else's problem, how's it all going to come together?

When I became CTO at the CMS, one of the first approaches to the position I took was to redefine what the role meant, particularly as it related to CMS and the challenges the agency was facing in the short- and long-term. I first met with key senior leaders in the agency to get their impressions and expectations for the role of a CMS CTO. I then started to reach outside CMS to other federal CTOs in the health-care industry and tech companies to first get their outside in view of the CMS CTO role, and then compare and contrast with their respective experiences within their own organizations. I didn't sit there and just assume the status quo that it was a scaled-down version of my predecessor's responsibilities. I wanted to know what other CTOs were doing inside and outside of government. And I knew that being a C-level executive comes with responsibilities and expectations for truly thinking on behalf of the larger set of issues at an enterprise level and the larger mission of serving people.

Being a public servant in the regular ranks means that you are working for the public and committing to improving how government works on their behalf. As a senior executive in public service, the shoes you are supposed to fill are even larger, because you now have to lead change and lead people, and do it in a way that considers the greater good, the bigger picture, the enterprise—and not just your respective area of responsibility. And in technology, you are supposed to work on solutions that do not create more technical debt, and in your spare time, work down that technical debt very creatively without going to OMB and asking for more money. (The answer would be no anyway.) The big shoes need to be filled with genuine commitment and selflessness. Without that, you would be haunted by your own half-hearted attempts to own it until something bad happened, or you would not even try anything risky, because certainly in government there are no rewards for taking risks. In your heart you would always know if you really gave the mission the effort it deserved. The minute you think you've arrived somewhere and you rest on your accomplishments, you'll notice that the shoes get a little bigger, and then you have to step up even more.

Working in CMS and being in the nexus of the US health-care system means there is always something you can do and always something you can improve. Standing at the end of my career at CMS and checking the line-of-sight back to when I first interviewed really bought into the fact that working at CMS meant that I was always only a degree or two removed from the center of an effort to improve Medicare, Medicaid, and other programs. If you choose to and you raise your hand to participate, no one will stop you. Sure, there are and always will be people who won't support you or are threatened by your lack of "collaborative spirit," but your efforts along with the collective teams you work on can really affect an outcome that's felt by the public and be able to change a small slice of health care for the better. Who wouldn't want that to be their legacy?

SILICON VALLEY—NOT NECESSARILY A PERFECT FIT

When it comes to technology, people often question, if it can be done in Silicon Valley how come the government can't do it?

There's a saying among people who work in the Medicaid program—when you've seen one Medicaid program, you've seen one Medicaid program. The federal, state, and local government staff, the vendors and contractors, and other stakeholder groups that are part of the overall Medicaid community share this saying because they have an appreciation for how the program has grown in size as well as diversity from state to state. Having an appreciation of the differences is key to understanding what you are working with and how much can realistically be done, particularly in very short time frames. Many of these major health-care initiatives require this appreciation, because there are no short-term entry and exit points for innovation—and this is because very few programs are implemented with a limited duration. Most programs are not designed with expiration dates except in highly specific and rare circumstances, so it requires dedicated teams with both short- and long-term strategies. Without that thought process, these projects that initially start with an infusion of leads who bring their tech savviness but leave in the short term puts these complex programs and projects in a quandary.

In my opinion, the jury is still out on the effectiveness of 18F/ Technology Transformation Services and the US Digital Service teams. There is no doubt that in concept these efforts are helpful and meaningful, but when you provide this kind of service on a temporary basis and do not, on any permanent basis, own the responsibilities beyond initial delivery, it will lose its effectiveness over time. It's like trying to speak a foreign language just like a native after taking four years of language classes without ever being fully immersed in the native culture.

Bringing innovation to government is not in itself a bad thing, provided that the great ideas are borrowed and implemented not only with the long view, but also taking into account the different elements that drive risk in adopting innovation. And, as discussed earlier, commercial entities have slightly different motivators than government. The public sector cannot eliminate old "products," it cannot replace old systems, so new must exist alongside the old. Unnecessary redundancy and duplication is the unintended result of agencies and programs receiving individual funding as part of a wide range of legislative actions that span time and policy domains. It's not difficult to see and point out the unnecessary redundancies across programs, but one must understand the origins that created this situation. Otherwise any efforts to fix things will be treating the symptom but not the disease. This is not an excuse, but rather a recognition of the reality one has to understand when developing, implementing, and integrating new products and services to support these programs.

There are numerous formal and informal arrangements to create public-private partnerships to maximize the best features that each organization has to offer, but with any public-private partnership, the private sector must understand the issues within the public sector: bureaucracy, procurement procedure, why a company is chosen, and the fact that checks and balances exist for other reasons within government—case in point, the regulations that recognize small businesses and created special programs to stimulate and create greater participation by small business in federal contracting.

With careful consideration of motivations, the relative value and constraints that each organization can bring to the table in public-private partnerships can certainly create a greater public good in the end. In fact, some public-private partnerships have proven to be good options when government incubates good ideas and then commercial interests take over to monetize those ideas, which then become a bigger public good. Think about the GPS in your vehicles…think about the Internet…

DIFFERENT DEFINITIONS OF SUCCESS

Public and private sectors have different definitions of "success" that can sometimes be at odds with each other. When the public sector creates a program to improve access to affordable health care such as the ACA, giving millions of people access to health care is a success for the public. When the private sector needs to streamline, cut expenses, and increase profits and shareholder value, a company might choose to drastically reduce or even eliminate employee benefits, particularly for their retiree population. In the private sector, taking such action can be viewed as a necessary option to exercise given how success is defined. Yes, it does improve the corporate profile, and the management team may even be rewarded for this action, but on the other side of the balance sheet are people who lose benefits.

In reference to the Insurance Marketplace, success is partially defined as "access to affordable care." But when a government entity partners with for-profit insurance companies to deliver access to those benefits, then at some point there must be the recognition that the strategy and tactics of a for-profit insurance company are largely about that—to make a profit. On the government side, in contrast, evaluating success is about how many people are removed from the uninsured column and can now be counted as insured, and whether that metric truly defines access to affordable care. Those are two very different ways to define "success."

While the Insurance Marketplace is not the typical example of public-private partnerships—given that there are different constraints, different motivating factors that must be considered for both public policy and private sector participation—there is a partnership in the sense that each side can fulfill their objectives if they participate in a fair and balanced relationship. And within that relationship, there has to be mutual appreciation even though the motivating factors and definitions of success are different. This is especially true when there are boundaries in which the government has to maintain responsibility and accountability for anything that is inherently governmental and ensure that those responsibilities and accountability are not diluted or delegated to nongovernment organizations without legislative or statutory guidelines and at least the establishment of explicit operating rules in a formal agreement and/or contract.

For example, determining the eligibility of an individual to qualify them for government-sponsored benefits such as health-care programs and/or subsidies furnished by the government to offset costs, such as with APTCs in the Insurance Marketplaces, is a governmental responsibility. Developing, implementing, processing, and storing all the sensitive data involved is rightfully managed by the government and its contractors (under specific provisions) and can't be crowdsourced and maintained by any organization that wishes to play in the mix and figure out their own model to monetize the value of being in the stream of processing and handling the data.

So while there may be a highly innovative approach to delivering certain needed functions and capabilities using public-private relationships, the innovation itself does not absolve the need to really understand the proper roles and responsibilities. Some may say that it's only developing software, and in a given situation the private sector may have the best talent, but that talent has to be harnessed (not constrained) under a contract or some formal agreement regarding roles and responsibilities, and that's largely due to the fact that in public programs, the government is responsible and accountable for protecting people's privacy and preventing unauthorized exposure of their sensitive data. Everyone wants the best talent involved in problem-solving. But a person who can problem solve using their vast developer experience and agile approaches is not necessarily going to have the critical thinking and problem-solving skills in, say, the Medicare context that's needed to do well in delivering a functioning system that fits well in the overall Medicare ecosystem and meets the requirements of federal laws and regulations that exist to protect people's information.

It can be very easy to lose sight of what is inherently governmental and not be vigilant in enforcing the boundaries while letting innovative practices and approaches be established in an unchecked manner. And innovation in technology and the skills in the use of technology are not the only factors for success. In addition to technical skills, a person would also need an appreciation and understanding of how the programs and policies currently work in comparison to how they will work with new policies and rules introduced. Only then will the technology component of the problem-solving process be meaningful and enable the expected changes.

Yes, it's good to bring in people who are experts in the technical domain and come from the private sector, but people who are already there know things, too. It's best not to defer 100 percent to others who are just stepping in the door because it seems safer to do so.

MAINTAINING SANITY UNDER PRESSURE

I recently had the pleasure of working with Steven Kelman and David Eaves from the Harvard Kennedy School, who teach a graduate level course titled "Preventing Digital Disaster: Why Digital Implementations So Often Go Badly." In the span of about two months, I had several calls with Steve to provide answers to some of his direct questions on aspects that contributed to such a poor launch of the Insurance Marketplace program. Steve and David graciously invited me to be a guest lecturer for the class, and I was more than glad to accept because I rarely turn down opportunities to meet people and explain some of the not so obvious or well-known aspects of working on projects like HealthCare.gov and to answer any questions. The challenge is always to have enough time and follow-up opportunities in these engagements to really have a conversation that informs all about what happened and what could be learned from the experience. There are a dozen or more rich case studies that can be done on the experience of taking on such a project from inception just after passage of ACA in March of 2010, through the day I retired from federal service in April 2015, and the project likely continues to generate great lessons to be learned since my retirement.

The people who are closest to me and know me often rib me about how I have this natural tendency to "hog the mic," and while that may be somewhat true, what truly inspires me—mainly the idealist in me—is to put the story out there. For all the good and bad, I have hope that some people will hear more than just the words and take it to heart that while every major undertaking such as HealthCare.gov will have problems and issues, the textbook version of what steps to take and what decisions need to be made will eventually encounter an immovable obstacle, and then you will have to completely reexamine what options are available in a critical, non-textbook situation. I am talking about considering options so drastic that they're akin to amputating a limb to save a life. I don't want to overly dramatize or take lightly situations where real people have to experience amputations, but over the years I've been exhausting the number of ways I can frame what reality was like between 2010 and 2015 working on HealthCare.gov and help others think about what they would do in similar situations and be ready for redefining options based on what can be a twisted reality.

As with the class I had the pleasure of lecturing at Harvard Kennedy and most every other engagement, I enthusiastically welcome questions such as: Why didn't you try to let your bosses know the dire conditions the systems were in? Why didn't you try to move the date so that you'd have more time to fix the issues? Why didn't you use more open source software? Why did you contract with companies that built proprietary custom solutions? Why didn't you use more agile approaches to software development? Why did you make everyone register for an account? I attempt to answer these questions and hundreds more by explaining what really happened, and most times I hear some form of follow-up that indicates that the frame of reference and value judgment is either textbook and/or based on not being able to understand the scale and complexity involved. And most importantly, many people do not factor in the instability caused by politics, particularly in the era of politics since the ACA was passed. Politically driven choice and decision framework defies logic. Some of the decisions made in rolling out HealthCare.gov seem irrational, because the options are calculated, created, and selected based purely on political calculus and not whether there will be a horrible user experience, which is contrary to the direction we received in the kick-off meeting I referred to back in 2010, where Dr. Emmanuel declared we would deliver a "world-class experience."

Post October 1, 2013, so many people who blogged, wrote articles, worked in the IT industry, and more were aghast at the horrible user experience, and used their respective frame of reference to opine on what happened and what should be done. Of the hundreds if not thousands of written pieces online and in print, only a few factored in the issues rooted in nontechnical factors that contributed to the situation at hand. When I am asked why the program rolled out the way it did, my immediate answer is: "It rolled out the way it did because that's the way it needed to roll out." And then I proceed to explain that answer by pointing to the nontechnical factors, such as the political landscape that influenced so much of how key decisions were made. Getting to October 1, 2013, was the starting line, not the finish line. Individually, the major reasons that contributed to what everyone experienced on October 1, both on the user side and the management side—namely delayed funding, delayed requirements, not enough time to adequately develop, integrate, and test, unwillingness to truly prioritize to create a viable MVP—all converged and were revealed. The sum total of all that should have been addressed earlier created a fireworks show that demanded everyone's fullest attention, and that's exactly what was needed.

Maybe I shouldn't use the word "pointing" in the paragraph above. Another unintended effect of explaining what happened is that somehow the story is interpreted as trying to point the finger at other causes. I have to be adamant that in sharing the story and possible lessons to be applied going forward, placing blame, deflecting blame, and trying to shine the light somewhere else does absolutely zero good. Setting the record straight might seem like an attempt at changing history, but how accurate and truthful history is depends on more than just one version.

It has been five years since the rollout and three since I retired, and I find the story of HealthCare.gov remains interesting to so many who just want to know what happened, and I am sure there will be many more classes, workshops, case studies, etc. that will include some version of what happened. I've tried to share my experiences and what happened from my frame of reference, including some of the history leading up to working on the Insurance Marketplace program, to try and explain that these major initiatives—such as transforming the health-care landscape for the better, in this case focusing mostly on getting health-care coverage for more people— was, is, and will continue to be endeavors that span decades, and that as each disruptive event occurs—such as the launch of HealthCare.gov, or when each open enrollment period comes and passes, or as new programs emerge on the landscape of health care—the difficult process of making it work is not definable by a single date or event. As public policy, we all have to periodically ask ourselves and our politicians whether things are truly improving in the US health-care system. If you don't like the answer, perhaps you can step into public service and try to improve things for as many people as possible.

If you do, always remember that in working on behalf of so many others, you have to know who you are and what you stand for, and be resilient and focused on what needs to be done, regardless of how bad the situation is and how bad the options may seem.

ACA: Affordable Care Act

AHIP: America's Health Insurance Plans

APTC: advance premium tax credit

AWS: Amazon Web Services

CCIIO: Center for Consumer Information & Insurance Oversight

CHIP: Children's Health Insurance Program

CIO: chief information officer

CMMI: Center for Medicare and Medicaid Innovation

CMS: Centers for Medicare and Medicaid Services

COB: coordination of benefits

CSR: cost sharing reductions

CTO: chief technology officer

DHS: Department of Homeland Security

DoD: Department of Defense

DSH: Data Services Hub

DUA: data use agreement

EA: enterprise architecture

EDI: electronic data interchange

EHB: essential health benefits

EIDM: Enterprise Identity Management System

ETL: extract, transform, and load

FAR: Federal Acquisition Regulation

FBDE: full-benefit dual eligible

FedRAMP: Federal Risk and Authorization Management Program

FEI: Federal Executive Institute

FFM: federally facilitated Marketplace

FPL: federal poverty level

GAO: Government Accountability Office

GSA: General Services Administration

HCFA: Health Care Financing Administration

HHS: Health & Human Services

HIPAA: Health Insurance Portability and Accountability Act

HITECH: Health Information Technology for Economic and Clinical Health

IaaS: Infrastructure as a Service

IRS: Internal Revenue Service

IV&V: independent validation & verification

MACRA: Medicare Access and CHIP Reauthorization Act

MITA: Medicaid IT architecture framework

MLR: medical loss ratio

MMA: Medicare Modernization Act

MVP: minimum viable product

OCIIO: Office of Consumer Information and Insurance Oversight

OGR: House Committee on Oversight and Government

OIG: Office of Inspector General

OIS: Office of Information Services

OMB: Office of Management and Budget

OPM: Office of Personnel Management

PCIP: Pre-existing Condition Insurance Plan

PCMA: Pharmaceutical Care Management Association

PHR: personal health record

PII: personally identifiable information

POS: point of sale

QHP: qualified health plan

RDBMS: relational database management system

RR: rate review

SBA: state-based Marketplace

SOR: systems of record

SSA: Social Security Administration

SSN: Social Security number

TANF: Temporary Assistance for Needy Families

TRA: technical reference architecture

TRB: technical review board

VA: Department of Veterans Affairs

WIC: Women, Infants, and Children